HR Analytic...

The What, Why and How...

Tracey Smith,
BMath, MASc, MBA

*If you can't explain it simply,
you don't understand it well enough.*

Albert Einstein

Copyright © 2013 Tracey Smith

All rights reserved.

ISBN: 978-1492739166

CONTENTS

ABOUT THE AUTHOR

Tracey Smith led the global strategic workforce planning initiative for FedEx Express World Headquarters. In addition, she led a variety of global, strategic HR projects where expertise in data-driven decision making was required. She educated HR on the value of analytics and demonstrated by example, the correlations which could be determined and the value which could be derived. She is now an independent consultant advising clients on analytics and workforce planning. Her clients span multiple countries.

Prior to her work for FedEx Express, Tracey spent 11 years in the automotive industry in Canada working for a Tier 1 supplier where she led an engineering team of analytical professionals. This team used their numerical analysis skills to predict, simulate and experimentally test new automotive products.

Tracey holds a BMath degree in Applied Mathematics and a MASc degree in Mechanical Engineering from the University of Waterloo, Canada specializing in numerical modeling. She also holds an MBA from Texas Christian University specializing in forecasting, operational analysis and supply chain.

Tracey provides a wide variety of consulting services to her clients in addition to providing on-site workshops and on-call advice. She has over 20 years of experience in the areas of Human Resources, Supply Chain and Engineering.

She was born in the U.K. and has worked in both Canada and the U.S. Her work helps others make better business decisions by utilizing strategic, data-driven techniques which focus efforts on those decisions which will yield the most value by establishing correlations between HR data and desired outcomes. Tracey is described as having one of the most numerical approaches to HR, a global view, and an uncanny ability to solve business problems.

Tracey presents on a variety of business topics at conferences, seminars and corporate workshops, primarily on HR analytics and its value to the organization. Her presentations combine strategic theory with real-world case studies.

Tracey is the author of several books which are available globally. A description of "Strategic Workforce Planning: Guidance & Back-Up Plans" can be found in the Appendix. Additional books can be found on her web site, www.numericalinsights.com, and on Amazon book sites worldwide.

Chapter 1: Introduction

As time has passed, more and more departments inside organizations have become data-driven in their decision making. When we think of departments like Finance and Operations, we can easily visualize those being highly analytical, but we don't often think that way about Human Resources.

Human Resources is one of the last departments to fully leverage its data. Sure, we've all seen the reports on turnover and the company that typically tried to address the localized areas where turnover was highest, but that's about as far as it went. The problem is that most people in HR came up through the traditional HR jobs where they are aligned to addressing the policy needs of the company and the concerns of the employees. Typically these Human Resource professionals do not come from analytical backgrounds and analytical backgrounds are required to derive value from HR analytics.

As an additional challenge, software and data system providers have never really made HR a priority. Applications for HR have been fragmented and the purpose has been more one of recording employee information, performance, turnover, etc. in separate systems rather than providing an integrated system across HR.

Well, the Human Resources world has been changing. Systems integrating employee information, job competencies, performance and succession planning are now available. Integrated learning management systems are also on the market. A shift in the skill sets of HR employees can be seen. Small analytical teams are appearing in the HR function to provide leadership with better insight with which to make decisions.

To understand this trend, an understanding of the evolution of data analysis is required. Years ago, the data produced within an organization would have been a report of "things gone by." Data systems were not real-time and extraction of data from computer systems was more difficult than it is today. As data systems evolved and computer capabilities increased, it became possible to store and analyze greater amounts of information. This provides the ability to move away from reporting a snapshot of times past. Trends over time can now be analyzed in order to see patterns of information and statistical techniques can prove or disprove relationships in the data.

As an organization moves through the evolutionary stages of data analysis, the value to the company increases. Data analysis provides management with a way to make better decisions.

Why has this become increasingly important to HR? HR is under pressure to become leaner and more strategic. Recent literature in the HR field has been concentrated on proving the value of HR to the bottom line and putting a dollar value on human capital. HR leaders are being asked to prove the value of new programs before they are allocated additional funds.

How can HR show value? This book is provided to guide you into the land of HR analytics to answer this question.

Who Should Read This Book?

The reader of this book is a business leader, an HR leader, analyst, student or just plain curious about what analytics in the Human Resource function is all about. In general, this book is intended for the business-minded individual interested in learning about the strategic advantages which can be obtained from performing analytics on the wealth of data stored in HR systems.

This book will not focus on convincing the reader of the importance of HR analytics. By purchasing this book, you've already recognized that HR analytics and strategic workforce planning are two of the hottest topics in HR. Likely you are an HR leader attempting to implement this function in your organization or you are an HR analyst trying to derive greater value from data analysis.

The book begins with a brief history of the evolution of HR information and explains some of the differences between the stages of information. It also provides an opinion on who needs to know these differences and who doesn't.

The book moves on to provide advice on how to best select metrics for HR and how to approach an analysis in an organized way.

Regression analysis is introduced as one of the most valuable mathematical techniques available for HR analyses. A full chapter is dedicated to practical examples in order to assist the reader in generating ideas of how to provide value to the organization. Examples are provided using simple and more advanced techniques. The intent, however, is to show where value can be found in HR data and not to provide instruction on mathematical techniques. Numerous books on regression analysis are already available.

For the HR leader, the book will go on to examine the advantages and disadvantages of trying to build these capabilities in-house and will provide a realistic view of the challenges associated with implementing analytics in Human Resources.

For the HR analyst, a section is included to discuss the realistic challenges you will face in collecting and analyzing HR data. Those entering this field or thinking about it, can then go in with their eyes wide open.

A brief introduction to Strategic Workforce Planning is provided because it overlaps with HR analytics in one of its major steps. For those wishing a more detailed description, please see the book "Strategic Workforce Planning: Guidance & Back-up Plans" described in the Appendix.

Finally, the book provides advice and opinions on data analysis and visualization tools available to the HR professional.

What Will This Book Do for Me?

Before the reader embarks on his / her journey through the pages of this book, it is important to know the types of questions that will be answered. Only then can the reader determine the true value of this material for his / her business.

The list below is not all inclusive, but will provide the reader with an idea on how the information contained herein can be used.

1. How can I show some HR analytics "quick wins" to my leadership team?
2. What are the evolutionary stages of analytics and in what stage are most businesses?

3. How can I organize my analysis efforts?
4. What can regression analysis do for me?
5. How can I link HR to the business?
6. How can I get strategic value out of an HR survey?
7. Should I have an in-house analytics group? If so, for which skill sets should I look?
8. What challenges can I realistically expect to face if I head into HR analytics?

Under the new pressure for Human Resources to provide higher value to the company, answering these and similar questions for the organization will increase the strategic level of Human Resources.

Chapter 2: HR Analytics

The Evolution

The use of analytics inside an organization has evolved at different speeds in different functional areas. Areas like Finance, Accounting and Operations have traditionally led the way as data has been easier to obtain through technology. Additionally, the employees within these areas have been "numerically inclined."

Technology systems for Human Resources have lagged behind because the demand for analytics was low. HR has traditionally been an area run more by gut feel than data. With the pressure on HR to now prove its value to the organization, this is rapidly changing. In recent years, economic necessity has pushed HR to embark on a journey to become more analytical and more strategic.

As we examine the informational evolution in HR, it progresses through several stages. Each evolutionary stage provides greater value to the business.

The evolutionary stages, in order of increasing value to the business, are:

1. Opinion-driven decisions
2. Reporting
3. Metrics, dashboards and external benchmarks
4. Predictive analytics
5. Strategically-aligned data analysis

An examination of companies across the globe will quickly demonstrate that the HR function is widely spread across these five stages. Very few HR teams still operate purely on opinion-driven decisions but an overwhelming number are still operating in the reporting stage.

Opinion-Driven Decisions

Thinking back to my engineering days in the late 1980s and early 1990s, I recall when all of the company's employees were gathered together to introduce everyone to a brand new machine. It was called a fax machine. At that time, we all shared one DOS-based, monochrome computer, had no email, and the PC was used primarily for printing data graphs. We used a ruler and a pencil to interpolate data and we made a judgment call on what would happen in between the data points. Was it linear? Quadratic?

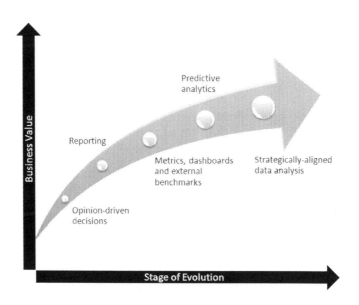

Figure 1: The Evolution of Data Analysis

While we had some data at hand, the available technology did not make high-level analysis possible. Many of our decisions, were opinion-driven or made on "gut feel." On the up side, since the situation was the same for our competitors, we at least had a level playing field.

Historically, the same situation has been the case for HR. The difference is that it remained that way much longer in HR than in any other functional area. The traditional backgrounds of those entering the HR profession do not include an education from a numerical field nor did the demands of HR require it. With advances in technology and economic challenges forcing the top executives to examine the value of HR activities to the business, this has changed dramatically.

Reporting

As the processing speeds of PCs began to double in short time frames, as memory storage rapidly increased and as software applications greatly improved, organizations moved toward reporting. Reporting consisted of data representing the past and answering the question "What happened?"

IT technology had not reached the point where data was available in a timeframe even remotely close to real time, so these reports were always a snapshot of the past. The norm of reporting was a series of overnight batch queries to a mainframe system followed by a series of manual data manipulations.

Many organizations are in the reporting phase today, but the barrier is no longer processing speeds and storage. Today's barriers include the ability to access real time (or close to real time) data and knowledgeable people to analyze and interpret the information properly. Additional barriers include the cost of technology solutions in volatile economic times. When it comes to budgets,

Human Resources is not usually the priority since it is not the core of any company and doesn't produce revenue. Financially, HR is a cost center and the priority is to protect and invest in the core operations of the company. How does an HR professional overcome the budget challenge? Using what you have, begin demonstrating the value of HR to your leadership.

Metrics, Dashboards and External Benchmarks

The next phase of evolution brings metrics, dashboards and external benchmarks. IT technology in this phase is advanced enough to make real-time or near real-time data available. This phase answers the question "What is happening today?" Many data visualization tools are available on the market today and they are improving at a rapid pace. There is certainly one out there for almost any budget, whether you want to create customized visualizations for the company or use a pre-set series of HR and business metrics.

What are metrics? Metrics are a series of measures tracked by the organization for the purpose of driving desired business behaviours or providing insights into what's happening inside the company. For HR, popular metrics include measures related to turnover, recruitment, training, performance and employee behaviours like absenteeism. Of greater importance in modern day is to relate these measures to the business' financial performance using metrics like revenue or profit per employee (or full time equivalent), cost of recruitment, cost of absenteeism and cost of HR as a percentage of revenue.

The examples of HR metrics above are just a sample. There are literally hundreds of metrics that relate to the activities within the human resources function. What then, is the key to selecting the right metrics for your company? Several guidelines for selecting effective metrics are given later in this chapter but the primary concept to keep in mind is to ensure that you align your metrics to your most pressing business issues. This means that the metrics you select for your company do not have to be the same as those of another company. Additionally, focus your efforts on a few high-priority metrics. An overdose of tracking metrics leads to conflicting directions and a lack of focus for employees.

Dashboards, on the other hand, are data visualizations that help employees make more informed decisions by representing the "bigger picture" all in one place. Generally, it is a graphical representation, although dashboards can be in tabular format as well.

Depending on the information depicted on the dashboard, these visualizations can make it easier to identify trends in information and to get a better overall view of the data. Dashboards do not necessarily have to be updated in real-time but are generally updated with regular frequency. The desired update frequency is really a function of what you're actually measuring. Does it change rapidly or slowly? Do you need to know the daily trending or is monthly or quarterly sufficient?

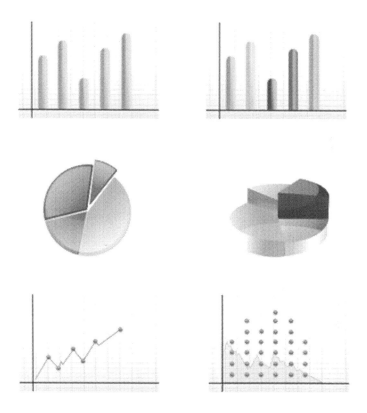

Dashboards usually group together information of a related nature. For example, HR may elect to group its turnover metrics together on one dashboard page or may choose to summarize HR metrics by department or geography. More sophisticated dashboards will provide the user with the ability to change these groupings at will.

As another example, a dashboard for your human resources group may include demographic data, succession planning information, employee mobility options, and bench strength summaries.

The final piece in this evolution adds an external benchmark value for important metrics so an organization can compare itself to other organizations. It is recommended that you exercise caution when using external benchmarks. How do you know that the company to which you are comparing yourselves is the level of excellence you wish to achieve?

Predictive Analytics

Advances in automating statistical algorithms within software applications such as Excel, MINITAB and SPSS give organizations the ability to consider "What will happen tomorrow?" This information is based on past trends and the mathematical expert needs to determine the best statistical model to represent the future. This is predictive analytics.

Techniques like data mining have become very popular. This technique seeks patterns within large data sets and answers questions such as "what is happening and where is it happening?" This allows predictive analytics to answer the questions of "where will it happen again and in what magnitude?"

Predictive analytics first proved its value in academic institutions and government. These environments typically have resources and budgets that can be dedicated to the development of new capabilities. Businesses generally have smaller research budgets and must dedicate more of their dollars to projects with a greater probability of contributing to the bottom line. The cost of these tools has declined over the years. Predictive analytics is now available to even the smallest of businesses since analysis no longer requires mainframe systems and can be performed on the common computer.

For the human resources function, predictive analytics now allow us to determine whether certain HR programs worked, whether they are worth continuing or whether we will never see a return on our investment even if that investment solely consists of time. It also allows us to statistically prove relationships between HR activities and operational metrics. Specific examples of these are given later in this book.

Strategically-aligned Data Analysis

Strategically-aligned data analysis takes predictive analytics one step further. In this stage, the business strategy drives the prioritization of data analysis and future predictions are no longer driven by past trends alone. A scan of the external competitive environment drives the need for several possible futures instead of one. We call these possible futures "scenarios" and the strategic analysis becomes that of scenario planning.

An excellent example of this is strategic workforce planning where the business strategy and activities on the near-term strategic plan will drive the scenarios for which predictive workforce models are built. This book will provide an overview of the steps involved in strategic workforce planning but for readers requiring a more in-depth look at this function, the book, "Strategic Workforce

Planning: Guidance & Back-up Plans" is recommended. A description of this book is given in the Appendix.

I've added this fifth stage as a reminder of the need for strategic alignment. As companies move through the evolution of HR information and data analysis, they frequently go overboard on the metrics, reporting and analytics. They fail to ask some important questions like: "What value will this provide?", "What actions can we take based on the results?"; "Does this support our strategic objectives?" Some companies analyze for the sake of analyzing and the result is wasted resources... something that no company can afford these days.

Do We Need to Know the Difference?

Now that we've learned the differences in the stages of information evolution, is it really that important to know the difference? Is it really that important for your internal customer to know the difference?

For the HR analytics practitioner and leader, the distinctions of the stages should be known as it allows you to assess the maturity level of your HR analytics, i.e., where are you in relation to where you can truly evolve this function? However, regardless of the stage, the following fundamental question needs to be foremost in your mind: **What are the biggest problems and how can HR contribute to their solution?**

For your internal customer, distinctions between predictive analytics and workforce planning are far less important. In fact, spending time explaining these differences may cause your internal customer to lose interest entirely. The only thing your internal leaders know is that they have issues and they need solutions. If you keep that fundamental concept in mind, you and your internal customers will be speaking the same language and have a better relationship.

How to Approach an Analysis

The thought of having to conduct an analysis strikes fear in the hearts of many HR professionals. Sometimes it's the fear of not knowing analysis techniques, sometimes it's the fear of what the data will reveal and often it is because they just don't know where to start.

Analysis techniques can be learned and there is no sense in worrying about what the data will reveal. It is what it is and your audience will either believe the result or not. With that said, I will address the topic of not knowing where to start.

The mindset for solving analytical problems is outlined in the following steps:

1. Determine the list of questions you are truly trying to answer.
2. Check the data.

3. Determine which analysis methods should be used.
4. Conduct the analysis and interpret the information.
5. Tell the story.

Determine the List of Questions You Are Truly Trying to Answer

Don't try to answer everything about everything. The simpler you can keep the problem definition, the better chance you have of remaining focused on the goals that are of value to the business. I've seen many analysts broaden their problem scope so much that they have no chance of answering the original question before the stated deadline.

Check the Data

This applies to two areas of analytical problem solving. First, something must have originally triggered the impression that an analysis was needed. Find out what this was and make sure that the data behind it is accurate. Very few people perform this check and nothing is more embarrassing than spending valuable resources on something unnecessary... except having to explain that to the company's executives. Document the data source from which this information was pulled and sit down with the person who originally pulled the data. I always have some doubt in my mind as to the accuracy of any information until I actually pull the same data myself. Seeing is believing!

The second area of data to check is the raw data that you will use for analysis. This is where the old saying of "garbage in; garbage out" comes into play. For large data sets, the best approach is to start by performing a graphical analysis.

A graphical analysis is nothing more than several graphical views of the data at a high level in order to see whether anything looks odd before you dive into more sophisticated analyses. If something looks unusual at a high level, you can spend time correcting the data before you spend large amounts of time analyzing inaccurate information.

If the data is accurate, performing this graphical analysis step can often tell a story about what type of insights can be found buried within the data set.

Determine Which Analysis Methods Should Be Used

Thousands of pages could be dedicated to the analysis methods available to the reader, but the important guideline is to keep it as simple as possible. Higher end methods are really cool to math geeks like me, but they are of no use if you can't explain what it means to the executives and their business.

Conduct the Analysis and Interpret the Information

I have paired these two tasks for a very important reason. I have met some people who can "run the numbers" but have little chance of figuring out what the analysis is trying to tell them. The value to the business is not in the numbers; it's in the message behind the numbers. Without this message, the business can't act on the analysis and hence can't derive any strategic value from it.

Tell the Story

There is one final step in this process and that is to figure out how to convey the message of the analysis. The interpretation of the data has to be presented in a format that the audience will understand. This is known as "telling the story."

What does the analysis mean? What recommendations can you make from what the data tells you? How will you explain the analysis methodology to prove that it is supportable? The ability to tell the story in a clear and concise fashion is a skill that few people possess. A great deal of thought and preparation is recommended. Most analyses take a fair amount of work to complete but fall short in conveying the results to the audience or convincing them that the analysis method is sound.

In most companies, this audience will consist of management team members. One mistake that people make when presenting to management is to assume that management is as familiar with the information as the person who conducted the analysis. This is rarely the case. For the person who conducted the analysis, the information is well known because they have probably been looking at it for days or weeks; the audience has not.

For me, the audience has been as high as the Board of Directors and the company founder. From what I have experienced, the higher up you have to present your analysis, the less time you have to convey your message. This is where my previous recommendation of being clear and concise really comes into play. At these levels, you have 10-15 minutes to convey your message. Make it an impactful one.

In summary, it is important to have an accurate analysis. Beyond the analysis, it is important to take the time to "tell the story" so that your audience can understand it... and for goodness sake, make sure your story actually answers the original business questions that prompted the analysis in the first place.

Metrics

Metrics are probably one of the simplest forms of business measurement because they require no heavy mathematical lifting but they provide a vast amount of insight when carefully selected.

Wouldn't you like to know which way your turnover is trending and whether it's increasing in only certain locations? Is it true turnover or is it the result of a retirement wave coming through the employee population?

Is turnover seasonal? Do people generally quit the company in July to have time to prepare for their kids to go back to school and then seek re-employment after the school year starts?

Simple metrics in HR can provide a great deal of insight. If we take a look at a metric like revenue per FTE (full-time employee or equivalent), we can quickly see if the employee population is getting out of line with revenue. We can take action to correct this as soon as possible. That said, I prefer metrics which relate to profit more than revenue and those which can attach a cost to the employee base.

To be successful with metrics, you need two things: good data sources and common sense. I told you it was simple! You've already demonstrated common sense by picking up this guide, so let's begin with some fundamental rules for selecting metrics.

The Fundamental Rules of Metrics

1. If you don't measure it, you can't manage it.
2. If you can't take action on it, why measure it?
3. People will behave according to the metrics and targets you select.

Let's discuss the logic behind each one of these rules.

If you don't measure it, you can't manage it.

This phrase has been in the vocabulary of management for decades and still holds true today. You should not make a decision based on what you *feel* is happening in your business if you have the ability to actually *measure* it. I have seen quite a few cases where leaders assign resources to unnecessary projects based on gut feel when it would have taken less than 30 minutes to look at real data and make a better decision. The result is a waste of precious resources.

If you can't take action on it, why measure it?

This is where common sense comes into play. I was once presented with a metrics dashboard for an organization. This was a large organization split into two groups. Let's call them Corporate Services and Operations.

The dashboard presented was for Operations. The problem was, the dashboard contained several metrics for activities which were controlled entirely by Corporate Services. If these metrics drifted off course, what was Operations going to do about it? Why would Operations waste resources having its employees gather data on a Corporate Services metric each month if they could take no action on the metric when it trended in an unfavourable direction? If this metric was important to the organization, then it belonged on a dashboard for Corporate Services.

People will behave according to the metrics and targets you select.

Peter F. Drucker once said, "What's measured improves." Employees pay attention to the measurements by which they are judged, especially those linked to their compensation. If you set a goal for an employee to achieve $1M in sales this year and he / she achieves that number in the first seven months, you may find that the employee coasts for the remainder of the year. As you select the metrics for your business, it is very important to dedicate a good deal of thought to the unintended consequences of these measurements.

As an additional example, if you set a goal for your recruiting staff to hire new employees within 60 days and they are finding this goal to be a challenge, the tendency will be to settle for lower quality candidates in order to meet the "time-to-hire" metric. As I have previously advised, for each metric you put in place, think about the possible unintended consequences. In order to counteract this behaviour, a "quality of hire" metric can be implemented. Quality of hire is a much talked about metric today. It has no set definition as the definition of what a quality employee is will depend on what is most important about these employees in your own organization and in a specific role.

How do you know if you are doing well?

To know if you are doing well, you need something against which you can compare your performance; you need a benchmark value. One of the best benchmarks to have is one from your own industry. If you are taking 90 days to hire an employee, is your competitor hiring within 60 days?

If a benchmark in your own industry is not available, try to contact a company in a fairly similar industry and roughly the same size. Chances are they would like to benchmark with you just as much as you want to benchmark with them. I have never had an issue locating willing participants as long as we all stayed within the confines of our confidentiality restrictions.

Further Advice on Metrics

A metric isn't useful unless people actually know about it. Communicate it to the employees and management.

Allow employees to help you select the right metrics. They are more likely to accept them if they had a hand in selecting them rather than receiving them as just another order from above.

Make sure employees understand why each metric was selected and what it means to the success of the business. Again, this is far more successful if the employees help select the metrics.

Keep the measurements simple so everyone can understand what it means when the value goes up or down. There is no reward for creating the most complicated metric. People on every level of the organizational chart need to have a clear picture of what you are measuring and why.

Less is more. It is easier for employees to focus on a few metrics than a dashboard of twenty or thirty. People cannot possibly focus on a large number of metrics and you will find that some may start to contradict each other in intent. You may also find that you will begin to affect the culture as employees start to feel like their every movement is being watched.

Make sure you review these metrics over time. The metrics you need for today's performance and today's business challenges are not necessarily the metrics you need to be successful years down the road. The world changes quickly and a review of the metrics you selected in the past is recommended every few years.

Lastly, don't be afraid to let go of old metrics. Many companies are so fearful of halting measurement on a metric for fear that "someone may ask at some time in the future." I once worked in a department like this and we probably spent about 20% of our time doing value-added work and 80% of our time reporting on it.

Regression Analysis

Regression analysis is about finding relationships in your data. It is a statistical technique used to describe the possible relationship between one variable and another. I consider it to be one of the most powerful tools available to an analyst.

Regression analysis has been very popular in other areas of the company such as engineering and operations. In fact, I was running regression analyses in engineering for the automotive industry back in the 1990s. Only recently, with the increased focus on implementing HR analytics, has regression started to become popular for HR studies.

Let's consider a popular question. Is engagement related to turnover? We go about our day-to-day HR activities under the assumption that it is true, but you can actually use regression analysis to prove whether this relationship exists for your company. You can also determine just how strong the relationship is. Knowing the strength of the relationship allows a company to say "If we increase engagement by 1%, we can anticipate turnover going down by x%.

While this is technically a statistical technique, there are many studies an HR professional can conduct without getting too far into the math.

Examples of questions which could be answered with this technique are:

1. Is engagement related to turnover?
2. Is the education level of the employees correlated with success in the job?
3. Is absenteeism correlated with the amount of time the employees have been with the company? In their current job?
4. Did a new sales training program actually increase performance?
5. Is the annual employee feedback survey correlated to turnover?
6. What are the common characteristics of people who fail in certain job roles?
7. Is the culture of the company correlated with operational performance?

Regression analysis is a way to determine if these hypothesized relationships hold true. In plain English, you can test to see if what you think might be true is actually true.

Regression models are used in a variety of business situations and can be useful in almost any functional area of the organization. Since this technique is about finding relationships between information sets, once a relationship is confirmed, it can be used for decision-making.

As an example: what if we want to know whether there is a relationship between the temperature outside and the sales of frozen drinks. We would define one variable in our data to be the sales amount and we would define a second variable to be the outside temperature. Collecting data over time would allow us to build a large enough data set in order to conduct a supportable analysis.

If we plot all of this data, a regression analysis would try to find the best line to represent the relationship between outside temperature and frozen drink sales. Once we have this line, we could then use it to forecast sales of frozen drinks by knowing the weather forecast.

As an additional example, suppose a training company approaches you and says that they have a class that all of your sales people can take which would increase their ability to find new customers. However, this training class is rather expensive. How do you know if it's worth the cost to train all of your sales staff?

Here's what you can do. Select a sample of your sales staff and train only that sample. Record the sales acquired by all of your sales staff for a time period before and after the training of the selected employees. If the training is as good as the training company promised, you should see the performance of the trained staff increase. You must also look at the sales data for the untrained sales employees to see if their performance also went up. If it did, then you cannot conclude that the increased performance seen in the trained staff was attributable to the training. Using regression analysis, you can take the set of data for all of your sales staff, flag the employees that received training, and a few regression values will decide for you whether any increase you see can be attributed to the training.

There are, of course, a few statistical items to check in order to validate that the model can be used for forecasting. We will forego a description of the technical parts of regression since that is best suited for a more advanced book. For the HR analyst and leader, it is sufficient to know that this technique is at your disposal and that the author considers it to be one of the most valuable tools out there.

As a final thought, wouldn't it be fun to negotiate with that training company such that you will only pay for the training if the statistics after the fact show that the training made a "statistically significant" difference?

The most commonly known form of regression is one in which the software tried to find a linear relationship between your two variables. As one of our simplest examples, you may seek to test whether there is a linear relationship between engagement and turnover. In this case, the software uses a least squares algorithm to find the best straight line to fit your data set.

If the reader is unfamiliar with the output produced by a regression analysis, sample outputs from Excel and MINITAB are shown on the following pages. The information presented conveys how well the two pieces of data you tested fit together on a straight line, i.e. how well does variation in one variable explain the variation in the other.

Excel is not a very convenient tool for running regression and my preference is to use a tool like MINITAB, but in a pinch, Excel will do the job. Where Excel becomes frustratingly inconvenient is when you want to run multiple variables in your regression analysis. It can do it, but it takes a lot more work to make it happen with Excel.

In reality, not all relationships will be linear. They may be quadratic, of higher polynomial relations, exponential, logarithmic, etc. For all of these non-linear relationships, an advanced book on regression analysis is recommended.

SUMMARY OUTPUT

Regression Statistics

Multiple R	0.539286211
R Square	0.290829617
Adjusted R Square	0.259996122
Standard Error	3.485253361
Observations	25

ANOVA

	df	SS	MS	F	Significance F
Regression	1	114.5736072	114.5736072	9.432262471	0.005403615
Residual	23	279.3807928	12.14699099		
Total	24	393.9544			

	Coefficients	Standard Error	t Stat	P-value	Lower 95%	Upper 95%	Lower 95.0%	Upper 95.0%
Intercept	30.02051706	7.323079843	4.09943872	0.000439346	14.87157221	45.16946191	14.87157221	45.16946191
X Variable 1	-0.284527223	0.0926243699	-3.071198865	0.005403615	-0.476175315	-0.09287913	-0.476175315	-0.09287913

Figure 2: Sample Excel Regression Output

Regression Analysis: Turnover versus Engagement

```
The regression equation is
Turnover = 30.1 - 0.285 Engagement


Predictor        Coef   SE Coef       T      P
Constant       30.058     7.325    4.10  0.000
Engagement    -0.28503   0.09268   -3.08  0.005


S = 3.48385    R-Sq = 29.1%    R-Sq(adj) = 26.1%


Analysis of Variance

Source           DF       SS       MS      F      P
Regression        1   114.80   114.80   9.46  0.005
Residual Error   23   279.16    12.14
Total            24   393.95
```

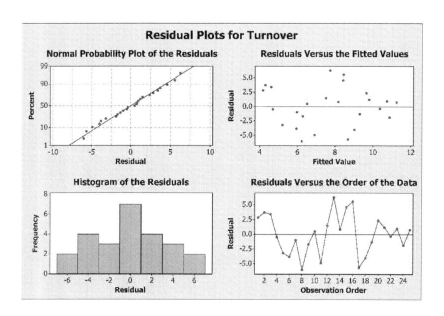

Figure 3: Sample MINITAB Regression Output

Chapter 3: Practical Examples

The Strategic Value in Surveys

HR surveys can be designed to be very simple or very complex, but they have one thing in common. They are conducted in order to gather information to answer a question that the company has in mind. Are our employees happy? Are our internal customers happy? Why are people leaving? What do employees think of upper management?

For some employees, the first survey experience when joining a company is when HR wants to determine the type of experience they had from their first day and even how they were treated during the hiring process. For those new to HR, this stage of employment is referred to as onboarding and the survey assesses whether the employee has entered the company with a good experience and within their expectations.

Ongoing surveys can come in the form of testing an employee's level of engagement, internal customer experiences, retention, culture, management approval levels and exit motivations.

What is the value in conducting surveys? Let's use the following case study as a demonstration of survey value.

How do you know whether your employees are spending their time on value-added activities? The following analysis helps to find these activities. Additionally, finding the non-value-added activities is valuable because you can then look at options to eliminate them, or use process improvement to automate or shorten the length of time these activities take.

A survey was developed to request the opinions of nearly 2,000 employees in a certain department. On that survey was a long list of the tasks that were involved in performing the job, a data field to enter the number of hours spent on each activity per week and a field from 1 to 5 ranking the importance of each of these activities for the business (in the opinion of the employees).

After the survey data came in, a great deal of number crunching obviously took place. The end result? A matrix like the one shown in Figure 4 which gives a great view into what these people do all day.

So what do we do with this information?

Well, look in the upper left corner of the matrix. These are activities that the employees are spending a great deal of time on but are of little value to the company. These activities should be put on a list for possible elimination, automation or process improvement to reduce the time spent on them. A prioritized list can now be provided to a team of improvement experts... and what better experts than the employees themselves? Teamed up with process experts, these employees have the greatest motivation to participate since the end result is a better work environment for them.

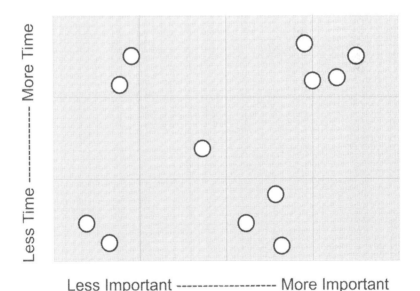

Figure 4: Assessment of HR Activity Value

For an added level of strategic analysis, consider one department such as Sales. Conduct the survey above with the employees of the Sales Department to determine which activities they think are of value to the customer. Next, send the same survey to your customers. Do your customers and Sales Department agree on what is of value? If they don't, Sales may not be spending its time on the most important activities. Remember, the definition of value is "what the customer is willing to pay for."

The same concept can be used with internal customers. Consider your Human Resources department. Conduct the same type of survey with your HR employees. At the same time, conduct an identical survey with the internal customers served by HR employees. Do they agree? I did this a few years ago in a large, global company and found substantial differences of opinion between what HR thought they should provide and what the internal customers indicated that they needed most. HR wanted to be on the path of providing more strategic services but the front-line workforce was more interested in the here and now services of HR. This is where you will need to balance the short-term and long-term needs of the business.

Assessing an HR Program

In this section, I will provide a short demonstration of how to determine which HR activities make a difference. Yes, I recognize that some activities will always be supported for regulatory compliance but what about the rest? Here are two examples.

I received a call from an HR Manager and the conversation went something like this. "Our leader told me that you can prove whether my coaching program was any good. Is that true? The employees' annual feedback scores went up, so it must have worked, right?" Of course, with that level of detail, the answer is "that depends...I will need a bit more information." With a few questions, the following background information was established.

HR had implemented a coaching program whereby HR reps coached operational managers who had the lowest annual employee feedback scores (AEF). The primary question on the table was whether the activity of coaching these managers had an impact on their AEF scores, essentially, did this program work?

To approach a problem like this, you have to isolate the impact of the program on the survey scores. Doing this is similar to how medical trials are conducted. In medical trials, a group of people are selected and only a subset of the group receive the drug being tested. The rest of the group receive a placebo. In our HR program example, we can obtain a list of the managers who were coached but also need a list of managers who were not coached. That way, the ones who were coached become our isolated subset of the population.

A regression analysis was conducted and, skipping the details of "statistical significance," whether the coaching activity was a contributing factor of the increased AEF scores was determined.

From this example, it is possible to assess whether a program had the right impact on your organization and whether you should continue to assign resources to it in the future. In this case, the company was fortunate that a metric existed by which to evaluate the program as they had not foreseen the need for one when the program was developed. It is important to determine a "success metric" before a program begins.

An additional benefit to this type of analysis is that the strength of the relationship between the AEF scores and the coaching program can be determined. This means that we can determine how much we can expect the AEF score to go up next year if an employee participates in the coaching program this year.

What was the true intent of the company in implementing a coaching program? Was it to raise the annual employee feedback scores? Not really. The fundamental assumption was that an increase in AEF scores would lower turnover in those areas of the company. Instead of assuming this to be true, why not prove it? The same mathematical technique can be used to prove whether the level of turnover under each manager is related to his AEF score. My point here is that as an HR analyst or HR analytics leader, ensure that you understand the fundamental goal behind the analysis. In this case, it was really to assess whether a new coaching program would be effective in decreasing turnover.

Engagement and Turnover

As previously mentioned, we go about our day under the assumption that engagement and turnover are correlated. Let's use this popular question and some sample data to demonstrate the value of causation. We will use a small set of data for demonstration purposes.

Suppose we gather together a set of engagement survey data recorded for each department and we match it up with their corresponding turnover rates. We begin our analysis with a simple plot of the data in order to get an overall view of the information. This is also a good way of finding out quickly if any of the data looks questionable.

Looking at the data, we don't see anything which would make us question the information. But, suppose we did. Suppose we had one point at an engagement score of 90 and a corresponding turnover rates of 27%. Would you find that odd? What do you do with this data point?

In data analysis, we would call this point an "outlier." It could be the result of one bad piece of information stored in our data systems but before you decide to throw that point out of your data analysis, you first need to investigate it in case it is actually found to be a real data point.

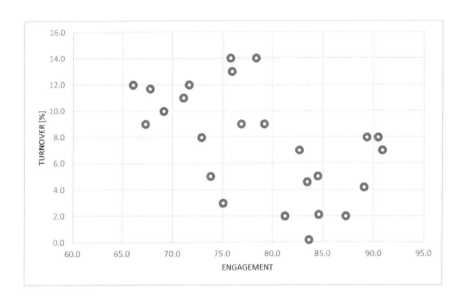

Figure 5: Sample Engagement & Turnover Data

To continue with our analysis, let's suppose that we determined that someone made a manual data entry mistake in our spreadsheet and that was the cause of our outlier. We have corrected our information and are ready to move on.

Running a regression analysis in Excel, MINITAB or SPSS, you obtain the output which is shown in Figure 6. This information tells us that engagement and turnover are indeed correlated and that the line of best fit is:

Turnover = - 0.2845 * [Engagement] + 30.021 .

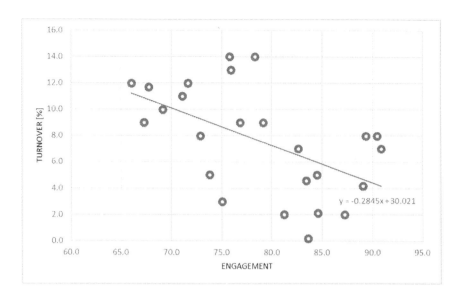

Figure 6: Line of Best Fit

The line of best fit is shown in the graph above overlaying our original data. The negative value in front of [Engagement] tells us that turnover and engagement are negatively correlated, i.e., as engagement goes up, we can expect turnover to go down. In fact, we can even say that every time the engagement score goes up by 1, we anticipate a decrease in turnover of 0.28%.

One point to keep in mind is that when you convey these results to your fellow analysts, you can certainly talk about t-values and p-values and r-squared. However, when you are conveying the information to people outside of the analytics world, keep the message as simple as "if this goes up by *this* amount, this other piece of information will go *up* or *down* by *that* amount." You can also convey how much variation of the data is explained in the model without having to explain the definition of r-squared or the various error measurements that regression analysis calculates.

You will notice that our actual data has a certain amount of variation from the linear approximation. That tells us that engagement is likely not the only factor affecting turnover. Other factors, both internal and external will account for additional variation. It is not necessary to account for all of the factors affecting the data. Often, it is sufficient to find one or more of the greatest contributing factors and to set forth actions plans based on those.

Causation or Coincidence?

I once led a large team of people who were delving into the root causes of unplanned absences. While proving many valuable correlations, one was very concerning. A statistically valid relationship was proven that said, "the more the manager is away, the less the employees are away." The team looked at me and said, "You're our leader so that means you get to be the one to convey this result to upper management."

As you can imagine, this result was met with great concern but having spent over 20 years in analytics, I know that not all correlations imply causation. This is when you need to investigate a little further before you conclude that this result is real.

In this particular case, we collected other data on the managers and took a look at how the employees responded on the managers' annual feedback surveys and any 360 surveys that had been conducted in the past. There was no evidence to support the hypothesis that the managers had any negative impact on absenteeism in the way the original correlation implied.

So, as a warning to those entering the HR analytics field, sometimes the data techniques will produce results that are questionable. Could this correlation have been real? Yes, it is possible but the only way to find out is to take the extra steps to determine what other data you can obtain to either substantiate or disprove the correlation.

Finding the Money in Analytics

Since we're on the topic of employee absences, let's use that as an example of "finding the money" with HR data. In this particular case, a company consolidated, from many different computer systems, the total number of days employees were absent during a year. The numbers shown in Figure 7 are fictitious in order to protect the confidential nature of the actual data, but suppose these values represent the total number of absent days for all employees, not for each employee.

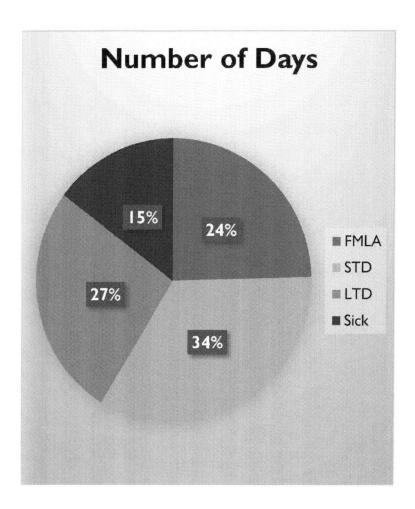

Figure 7: Total Number of Days Absent

In reality, the company also has a lot more categories of absenteeism so this example has been simplified for demonstration purposes. The categories represented are:

- FMLA: Family Medical Leave,
- STD: Short-term disability,
- LTD: Long-term disability,
- Sick: The employee phones in sick.

In order to save the company the most money, which category of absence would be the most significant? Would it be short-term disability because it has the largest number of days?

It's a bit of a trick question since money is not represented on the chart. We cannot assume that one day of sickness costs the company the same amount of money as one day of short-term disability. So, the cost to the company of one day of each of these categories of absence needs to be determined in order to translate this graph into money. A sample plot has been given in Figure 8.

With this type of information, you can now determine which type of absenteeism is costing the company the most money and therefore where the effort should be applied to reduce the cost. As a reminder, this data is fictitious and should not be used to derive any conclusions for your own organization.

The next step in the project was to align these absences with other HR data in order to test for correlations. The team investigated the data by location, average age of the employees, the length of service, and many, many more. By studying this information, we were able to prove several correlations.

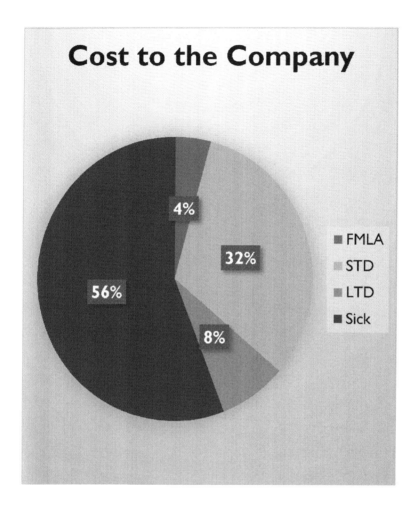

Figure 8: Cost of Absences

While all of the results cannot be presented here, we can say that the employees in the warm, coastal regions seemed to be absent on Fridays and Mondays more than non-coastal locations. This wasn't really a surprise to the management of those locations.

Dispeller of Myths

For the HR analyst and leader, you will find that part of your role will be to "dispel myths." That's not to say that you should make it your focus to go around the company pointing out how wrong people have been because they haven't looked at the data, but you will find that there are perceptions on certain topics that will need to be investigated and corrected.

Remember, HR does not come from a practice of looking at data to make their decisions. Recognize that they come from a history of gut feel and intuition for making decisions about HR programs and what they think is happening in the company. It will take quite a few analyses to slowly change how HR employees think and to guide them to investigate what the data is telling them before they move forward.

As an example, I sat in a meeting one day where the head of HR was asking his management to ramp up their activities of exit interviews because "we're losing so many people from HR these days." After a while, I asked him, "How do you know this is true." He began to list the names of people who had recently left. I then let him know that I had seen the turnover numbers recently and, in fact, the turnover in HR had declined three years in a row. The leader perceived that a large number of people were leaving HR only because, by mere chance, several people whose offices were close to his had all left HR within a two week period. His mind assumed that the rate of departure of people near his office extrapolated to the whole department. The numbers did not support that assumption. This is one case where, without the data, precious HR resources would have been dedicated to an unnecessary project.

A second example was a leader who came to me and said that the problem in his area of the company was that his specialized engineers were so much older than the rest of his organization. One quick graph was all that was needed to see that his specialized engineers were no different than the rest of the employees. In this case, we could put away any potential actions which would have been specific to those engineers and focus on his organization as a whole.

You will also need to dispel myths that come from outside sources. As an example, we received an HR newsletter that reported the fact that turnover was up 10% over the last year. One HR leader began to circulate this newsletter and began a discussion of possible actions. These newsletter numbers are built around surveying certain companies and rolling up the numbers to provide an average. The factors affecting turnover are numerous and you should not expect your company turnover rate to behave like the general public. It took less than five minutes to pull turnover data for the company and see that it had gone down, not up. Again, it will take a long time to train HR employees to look at data before they head off taking action on what they assume to be true.

Linking HR Data to Operational Performance

Let's take a look at another example. Consider the same employee feedback survey previously mentioned. Historically, HR felt that the higher these scores, the higher the level of performance for the company. With access to data, it was time to prove whether this annual feedback survey really had any impact on operational performance. Approaching the head of operations, we requested the selection of a metric within his area which he considered to be a "definition of success." He selected several and we were on our way.

With a little data crunching and statistics, all was known. Now the company could determine whether the programs associated with trying to raise annual feedback scores would actually produce an increase in operational performance, at least for the operational metrics selected.

What does this mean exactly? If the results showed that the annual feedback scores were correlated to the operational metric, HR could clearly say that "for an HR program that successfully increases the annual feedback score by 1%, we can anticipate an increase of x% in the operational metric.

However, if the results showed that the annual feedback scores were not correlated to the operational metric, that means that you can implement all the HR programs you wish to increase the annual feedback scores but it won't impact the operational metric at all.

This next example crosses the line between HR analytics and strategic workforce planning and does not require any knowledge of regression analysis. A decade ago, I did an analysis of a company's sales and determined just how much of their sales came from their top customers. This allowed the company to segment their customer base into A, B or C customer designations, with A being the top group in terms of revenue. The company then adjusted the level of customer service effort for each customer to match the segment in which the customer resided. A customers received more personalized treatment whereas the customer service for C customers was outsourced.

In the same respect, the products which were offered by this company were segmented by the level of contribution to the overall profit. The same A, B or C designation was used. In this case, A products provided larger contributions to the overall profit and on the opposite extreme, C products produced a negative profit. The company then adjusted their product strategy to eliminate C products by discontinuing them or adjusting the price to the market.

We can perform the exact same analysis on people. We categorize this under HR analytics but it's absolutely no different than analyzing products and customers. The technique is the same.

One job role that almost every business contains is the sales representative and it would not be uncommon for a company to track the sales brought in by each rep. Let's take a look at a company that has 48 sales reps and generates $42.3 M in sales. If we examine the amount of sales generated by each rep and sort them from highest sales to lowest sales, we get a chart which looks like Figure 9. We can quickly see that the top 12 sales reps are outperforming the rest of the sales force.

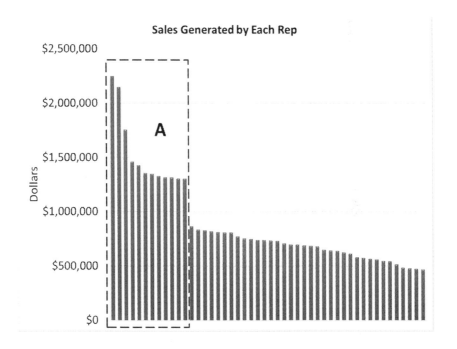

Figure 9: Sales Generation

Let's call them the A players. The remainder of people in this role seem to generate sales within a fairly similar range. We can call the remainder of these employees the B players or if the company sets a specific minimum sales generation goal for this job, we may further segment the employees to include C players, i.e., those falling below the minimum goal.

Now let's take a look at each quarter of the workforce. Since we have 12 A players out of 48 sales reps, that's the top 25%. Let's see how each group of 12 employees contributes to overall sales generation.

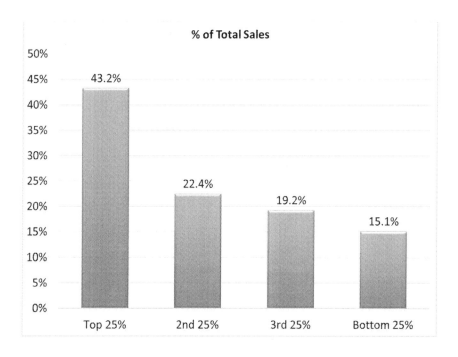

Figure 10: Sales for Each Quarter of the Workforce

Our A players represent 25% of the workforce but are producing 43% of the sales. In contrast, the bottom 25% of the sales reps are only producing 15% of the sales. Wouldn't it be great to now assess the characteristics of the top 25% to see what they have in common? Do they have similar personality traits? Do they excel in certain job competencies more than the bottom 25%? This is where you can take HR analytics even further.

Let's go another step further and overlay each employee's latest performance rating. This company uses a whole number rating scale of 1 to 5 where a 5 is the best score. The results are shown in Figure 11.

Figure 11: Sales Generation vs. Performance Rating

We would anticipate that the more sales a rep generates, the higher his / her performance score would be. For the employees on the upper end of this chart, this seems to be true. For employees below the $1.5M sales level, we begin to see a wider spread of performance scores. Below the $1M sales level, we see an even wider spread.

Before we jump to conclusions and start announcing to our leadership that the performance numbers don't make a lot of sense, the following discussion serves as a lesson in proper interpretation of results. We must put further thought into what we observe and think about the logical reasons of why this data is what it is. It doesn't take long to come up with possible reasons for the spread of performance ratings on the left half of the chart.

It is unlikely that the amount of sales generated is the only factor against which a sales rep is judged. His performance review likely has other factors like whether he performs well with his team, whether he has completed training goals, whether he shows a good understanding of the overall business etc. Therefore, you could have an employee who generates $1.5M in sales but can't get along with his coworkers. On the other hand, you could have an employee who has very low sales because he's only been in the job for six months, but he shows great initiative and works well with others. Only an examination of the performance review factors and their respective weightings will tell you how much spread in these scores can be reasonably expected.

Sales is a measurement which can be used for these types of analyses but one caution I would like to mention is that profit would be a more informative study. It is easier to generate sales at a lower margin than a higher one. Looking at the top sales, we can't really tell whether those sales are profitable. However, in reality, it is often difficult to obtain profit data whereas sales information is readily available in most companies.

You will notice that I have placed this example in a section called "Linking HR Data to Operational Performance." For the job category of a sales rep, the metric is financial but for other job categories, you will not have a direct link to a dollar value. For example, if you examine jobs in accounting, your operational metrics may be something like the number of transactions for accounts payable and receivable. Jobs on the manufacturing floor may be linked to production volume rather than the sales value of that volume.

I mentioned previously that this example crosses the line between HR analytics and strategic workforce planning. Strategic workforce planning is explained in Chapter 7 but at a high level, it is about segmenting the workforce in order to dedicate more resources to studying the critical roles in your company. For most companies, since sales employees generate revenue and have front-line contact with the customer, this job category normally lands on the critical role list. Once this analysis is performed, strategic workforce planning would drive actions such as disproportionately investing in these employees, prioritizing them in recruiting efforts and providing them with a different compensation strategy than that which exists for non-critical roles.

HR Data and Stock Performance

There are several brave consulting companies and individuals out there that have attempted to prove a statistical correlation between stock prices and HR metrics. Trying to correlate stock performance with the amount of money a company invests in its human capital is one example.

However, given the large swings in stock prices that we have witnessed in recent years due to the impact of global events and instabilities, it is clear that external forces beyond the control of corporations are having more of an impact on stock price than internal events. For that reason, it is up to individual companies to determine whether such a study on their own stock price over time would yield a return on the investment required for this type of project. It is more likely that an ROI can be substantiated on programs that are internal and where the impact can be isolated and measured more easily.

To date, it is more often the academic and research world that has taken on this challenge rather than the corporate world. Some impressive work on this topic certainly exists and is worth reading, but for the HR leader, it may need more development before it starts to become a mainstream HR activity.

There is also the issue of applying general results to your own company. As an example, it seems that there are HR articles released every day providing professionals with guiding results. In a previous example, I mentioned the article which reported that companies had seen a 10% increase in turnover. Before you act on this information, keep one question in mind.

The question is "how do you know this is true for your company?" It is fine to use these articles to get ideas on what to investigate in your own data, but don't take action and dedicate resources to issues before you have proven that they exist for you. In the particular case above, the company's turnover had actually gone down, not up, primarily because of their geographical location.

And So Much More

The specific studies in HR that can be conducted are far too numerous to mention. I could go on with example after example but I do promise my readers that my books will stay around 100 pages to accommodate the busy schedules of HR professionals. Essentially, if you track it; you can study it. If you don't track it and want to study it, you can certainly be creative enough to figure out how to record it or record something closely related to it.

Learning from others, let's take a look at some of the HR analyses that have been conducted and reported in the public literature from some of the big name companies.

Lowe's reported studying the relationships between employee engagement, compensation, managerial effectiveness, and store sales over time. The company now has a statistically valid model that helps top executives make decisions about leadership, organizational structure, and training which they have proven to have a substantial impact on store sales.

Molson Coors proved that engaged employees were 5 times less likely than non-engaged employees to have a safety incident and 7 times less likely to have a lost-time safety incident.

A study of 23,910 business units compared top quartile and bottom quartile engagement scores and found that those in the bottom quartile averaged 62% more accidents.

ARAMARK, a large food service companies, proved a relationship between OSHA (Occupational Health and Safety Administration) reports, employee satisfaction, and other variables on client renewal and upgrade rates.

A large insurance company has developed a set of statistically proven measures that help the company hire high-performing sales people. They found many non-obvious factors which correlate to strong sales performance and have now changed their screening criteria and raised first-year productivity by over 20%.

These are just a few of so many analytical possibilities for HR, so gather the team together, build your own project priority list and start to prove the connections that can be found inside your business.

Chapter 4: Data Challenges

After more than twenty years in the world of analytics and spanning the functions of engineering, supply chain and human resources, one of my most frequent pieces of advice is to "expect to be surprised." Nothing in the land of data is ever how you would like it to be. If you find that frustrating, then analytics is not for you.

A wealth of data exists in the Human Resource function. Most companies have the following information as a sample but not all inclusive list of HR data:

- Training records,
- Employee compensation,
- Information on a variety of benefits,

- Employee information (demographics, job codes, service years),
- Employee performance data, and
- Absenteeism records.

Challenges can exist as a result of all of these systems in addition to the interaction of these systems with one another. This chapter will outline some of the most common challenges you will come across in the land of analytics. The challenges discussed here are:

- Awareness of the data systems,
- Access to data systems,
- Missing data,
- Unknown definitions,
- Technology challenges, and
- Acceptance of results.

Awareness of the Data Systems

When you enter the world of analytics, you will quickly learn that finding the right data and preparing the data for analysis takes far longer than the analysis itself. If you have been working in an HR capacity for quite a few years, then perhaps you are more familiar with the data systems available. However, more often than not, unless a person has had a need to use a data system, they are probably unaware of its existence. Additionally, many analyses will require access to data outside of the HR function particularly when trying to connect HR data to financial or operational performance.

This is where awareness of existing data systems comes into play and relationships with employees in other functional areas is incredibly important. When you embark on an HR analytics project, you will need to put some thought into the goals of the project and the data needed to support it. If you need data outside of the HR function, it is recommended that you involve members outside of HR at the beginning of the project. If you help these people understand the goals and benefits of the project, they are more likely to help you. When you hold your project launch meeting, be sure to address the question of "what's in it for them?" especially if substantial effort will be required on their part. If you have strong, long-term relationships across the company, addressing this question becomes less important as those people are more likely to assist you just based on your credibility and reputation.

Access to Data Systems

In some companies, permission to access certain information is highly restricted, especially when it comes to financial systems and employee information. This makes it challenging to calculate even a simple metric like revenue per FTE (full-time employee or full-time equivalent) without the involvement of the Finance team or key financial person. Protecting the release of revenue data is understandable, especially if the company is public.

In one company, an effort to produce reports on metrics relating HR data to financial data was greatly delayed because the Finance team would not allow HR to pull revenue data. Therefore, HR had to wait for the Finance team to pull the information each quarter and send it to HR. HR then calculated certain ratios relating the revenue to HR activities. The Finance team then insisted on approving the calculation of these ratios.

The intent was to share these ratios with the leader of each division each fiscal quarter. Unfortunately, since providing revenue information to the Human Resources team was not the Finance team's highest priority, by the time the data was received, and HR created its reports, and Finance provided its approval of the final reports, the information was so out-of-date that it wasn't worth sharing with the divisional leaders. In this case, the effort to provide these metrics eventually died.

Access to systems sometimes comes down to the level of comfort that leaders have in individuals extracting and analysing data in a knowledgeable way. In some companies, the Finance staff have statistical knowledge; in others, their knowledge doesn't extend beyond the math needed for financial statements. In HR, there may be some employees knowledgeable in statistics if a specialized analytical group exists, but these employees are not typical.

Missing Data

While consulting to a company on a strategic workforce planning activity, where the fundamental goal was to create a mathematical model to predict future headcount needs, the client mentioned that they did not have the ability to get historical headcount information by job area. They tracked historical headcount as an overall number but could not separate that information by job category or department. This added to the challenge of the project since historical trends in each area of the company are valuable when trying to project patterns forward. In this case, we asked the leaders of the functional areas how long they had been with the company. We were lucky in that the majority of functional area leaders had substantial tenure with the organization and felt that they could provide an estimate of historical information for their areas from memory.

You will not always be lucky enough to find an instant solution to missing data. If not, it is recommended that you assess how important this information will be to the company in the future and if that value is high, set a plan to put a tracking method in place to start collecting that data. For the company mentioned above, since they could obtain real-time employee data by job category, they have begun to store snapshots of the workforce to start building historical information.

Unknown Definitions

Have you ever been in the situation where you have an endless supply of data available to you but no-one can tell you what the fields of data represent? Looking at one, very large HR data system, I had access to over 200 different fields in the database, but it was impossible to discern the difference between some of the fields. Even after enquiring with the personnel that manage the database and whose job it is to run reports off this database, even they couldn't tell me.

As an example, there were three fields that were called salary1, salary2 and salary3. Each had a different value but there was no data dictionary to tell me the definition of each field. Getting creative, I did manage to get one employee to share their base salary with me so I could find it in one of those fields. So, the mystery was solved on one of the three fields but no-one will likely ever figure out what the other two were. Scale that up to the number of issues I had with a 200-field database with no definitions and you can start to see the importance of recording data definitions. After three downsizings, I am certain that anyone who once knew this information had long since departed the company. Consider this as a warning of things to come if your company is undergoing substantial financial challenges or the wave of baby-boomer retirements is upon you. Documentation of Human Resource Information Systems (HRIS) is not a fun task but the information can certainly come in handy.

In this same category, i.e. a challenge with knowledge of what is truly contained in a data system, we once had two people provide an answer to an executive seeking a report. Not knowing that the request had made it to two different people, these two people submitted separate reports and the numbers didn't match. Now the issue you have is that the executive has no faith that HR knows what it is doing or how to get one version of the truth. In this particular report, headcount in the United States was the topic of the report. Inside the data system, the company stored not only the people that were part of the U.S. workforce but the people who worked in the Latin America division who were housed in the U.S.

One person reporting the data had removed the Latin America headcount and the other had not.

Technology

Here, I would like to offer a few points on the challenges of getting good data as they relate to technology. If you find that your data is spread across the company and it must be merged from several systems before you can even think of analysis, you are not alone. Almost every company is experiencing the same challenge.

It is common for large companies to have grown by purchasing other companies. With those new companies come a different set of data systems. The challenge of migrating all of the data from the purchased company into the central company often takes years and comes at great expense. Depending on what type of data it is, sometimes it doesn't make financial sense to undergo a project to consolidate this data.

This is actually one place where a smaller company has an advantage. Likely the number of data systems involved is fewer and far less complex than that of a larger company. However, with smaller companies, it is more likely that smaller, individual systems have been purchased over the years to accommodate new HR needs as the company grew or the company has done its best to build a home-grown HR module within one of its other systems. It is far less likely that a company this size has invested in an enterprise-wide HR system. Further, there is no one HR system that will meet all of your needs as the software in this area continues to evolve.

Regardless of the number of systems you will need to access in order to gather data for your HR analytics project, you will meet the challenge of compatibility. First, how will you export data from the multiple systems so you can use it? When you do manage to export the data, what amount of effort will be required to put it in a usable format? Since at least one common field is required to merge data from two disparate systems, is that field compatible?

As a practical example of this, suppose you want to do some sort of compensation analysis to see the variation on compensation as it relates to an employee's years of service with the company and the number of years in which they have been in their current role. Now suppose that the list of employees and their service with the company is stored in one database and their years of service in their current role is stored in another. In order to put these two sets of data together, both databases will need to have a common field.

Let's suppose that common field is the employee number and let's look at employee number 123456. In the first system, you find that the employee's number is stored as the number 123456, essentially one hundred and twenty three thousand four hundred and fifty six. In the second system, you find the employee's number is stored as "123456" or "00123456." This means the number is stored as a series of text characters and any attempt to match these two data systems will yield an error. The solution to this is a conversion of the data to either both be numbers or both be text but the point is that even the smallest incompatibility is going to yield additional steps in putting your data together.

The above example doesn't require a lot of extra work, but the following example requires a bit more. Suppose both systems store a state or province as text, but in one system it uses the full name and in the second system, it uses a two to three character abbreviation. Now you will need to construct an intermediary table for translation of text equivalents from one system to the other.

My advice to the new HR analyst, especially when mapping out project timelines, is to assume that putting the data into a consolidated set ready for analysis will take longer than you think. Experience in this area will allow you to make better time estimates for future projects and accessing the same systems in the future, you will already be aware of some of the challenges you will face when merging this data.

Acceptance of Results

This particular challenge is not so much about the data as the people receiving the analysis results, but I wanted the HR analysts out there to have an accurate picture of situations you might face.

Recalling that the final step of an analysis project is to "tell the story," it is rare, but sometimes the challenge you will face is that the story is not accepted.

Here is an example. A new program was implemented in HR to improve the performance of a certain job category. The idea for the new program came from a member of the leadership team.

The metric to measure the success of the program was determined and data on this metric was collected before and after the program. The analysis was conducted in just the same way as many before it, but when the regression results came in, the results showed that technically the program was "statistically significant," but in terms of the strength of the impact, it was as close to zero as I have ever seen.

What do you do with these results? As far as I could tell, the second half of the results were never really communicated and the program continued as if it had worked. To the HR analysts reading this book, I'm afraid that there really isn't much you can do in this situation. Move on to the next analysis and go in search of true value for the organization.

In other cases, acceptance of the results may be merely a result of the audience's acceptance level of the raw data used in the study. In this case, a discussion of data reliability and what can be done to improve it in the future would be my best recommendation. If you find yourself in this situation, rest assured, you are not the only company facing this challenge.

Chapter 5: Building the Capabilities

Should you Build the Capabilities In-house?

One of the most difficult decisions for HR leaders is whether or not to build analytical capabilities in-house. Very large companies like the Fortune 100 tend to say yes to this question more often than smaller companies and their challenge is more about where inside HR they should align this function.

A popular location to add HR analytics is with existing resources that execute employee surveys. The logic behind this is that the skill sets for analyzing company surveys tend to have a statistical component so these employees are familiar with data and analysis techniques. For companies who add HR analytics after adding strategic workforce planning, the popular locations are to link these employees to recruitment or to house them as a completely independent HR team.

For companies smaller than the Fortune 100 that are considering whether to build an analytics group in-house or whether to hire a consultant, there are several factors to consider. First, how urgent are the issues for which HR analytics are the potential solutions? If the urgency is high, you definitely need an analytical consultant in the short-term while you build your in-house team. This will provide support on your immediate challenges and this consultant can also provide guidance on how best to build and hire a team.

Another factor to consider is the volume of analytical work anticipated. Is this substantial enough to justify the cost of a full-time hire including employee benefits? Can you keep a full-time person busy at all times of the year? If not, the consultant option provides the ability to address volatility in workload levels and provides flexibility in your workforce.

Hiring Analytical Employees

If you conclude that the analytical workload in your business is sufficient to warrant building this skill set in-house, your next challenge comes in hiring analytical employees. Typically, people with analytical skill sets are very detail-oriented but also rather introverted. You will need to locate that rare person who has the analytical mind but can also speak to your management in terms they can understand. Additionally, they need to understand your business, your strategy and your company history instead of just understanding human resources. All of these areas will impact the approach needed in order for any analyst to tell an accurate story.

If you are building a dedicated group for analytics, you will likely not be able to hire enough people that have the analytical skills, an outgoing personality and the business savvy to make good decisions. In this case, it is recommended that the group be comprised of both types of analysts and that the business savvy analysts be the front face to management.

It should also be noted that there are several skill levels in analytical employees. I often find employees who are analysts by job title but not by function. The lowest level of these employees is the analyst who reports data but does not have the ability to interpret the information. The next level is the analyst who can interpret data and tell you how the numbers are trending, but they cannot relate it to the rest of the business and decision making. The highest level is the employee who understands the business and can make recommendations affecting the future of the company. We call this employee the "strategic interpreter." These individuals are a rare and valuable commodity.

The Analytical Leader

Many of the challenges in hiring the analyst are echoed in the challenge of hiring an HR analytics leader. Many companies have tried to promote from within, but often the personalities of the highly-detailed analyst do not translate well to a leadership role. The pursuit of perfection which exists in many of these individuals leads to micromanagement of the analysts, and micromanagement leads to employee dissatisfaction.

Many HR teams have promoted a member of their survey team which is usually an Organizational Psychologist. Often this can work well, but if this leader has spent their entire career in the HR field, they may not have enough understanding of the business to guide decision-makers.

The analytical leader has a background in a numerical discipline, perhaps mathematics, finance or operations. This will prepare them for understanding the work performed by the analysts. However, the leader should not have spent their entire career in one functional area. Experience in multiple functional areas will better prepare the analytical leader to view key business problems from several points of view. Often, what is optimal for one area of the company will be to the detriment of another area. Possessing a broad experience will prepare the leader for the compromises in solutions which inevitably must occur.

In today's world, the analytics leader needs to be interested in technology. Obtaining benefits from data analysis relies heavily on good data and flexible analysis tools. Part of the leadership function for an analytical group is to keep up to date on rapidly changing IT technologies and investigating which technologies will work best to solve the company's analysis challenges. A leader who has no interest in databases, analysis tools and visualization tools will not be successful. HR data technology has come a long way in just a few years, migrating from stand-alone applications to server applications and now into cloud computing. A review of some of these tools can be found in Chapter 6.

The next skill that you should look for in an analytical leader is their ability to form relationships within the organization. Most business problems require that data be gathered from several functional areas. Take as an example, the simple HR metric of revenue per employee. While HR owns the data system housing the employee information, the revenue data would be housed in a financial system. Often, HR will not have access to this system and must rely on the cooperation of the Finance team.

The final skill required is leadership. Combining the skill sets above in such a way as to envision the road ahead is how a company will derive strategic benefits from HR analytics.

The Challenges and Realities of Building In-House Analytics

I would be remiss if I did not provide the challenges and realities of trying to build an in-house analytics team or a center of excellence. I have attended many conferences where presenters provide the theory and approach for putting this type of team together but don't provide you with a list of the challenges that come with it.

Some of these challenges can be substantial enough to halt the plan altogether.

The first challenge is to convince your leadership that there is enough of a business case to justify the headcount, equipment and training required just to get this team created in its infancy stage. Many companies hire only the leader of the HR analytics team and the first task of the new leader is to assess the headcount and budgetary needs of the group.

Another challenge of building an HR analytics function is credibility. While forming this team, if it can't produce quick successes to prove the capabilities of the team, it is unlikely to receive additional funding to grow the team.

A lack of "quick wins" may not actually be a reflection on the team's capabilities. The team could fail on the quality of the data it used to make its analyses. This data quality challenge should not be underestimated. If the team is fairly new, the employees may not have enough experience using certain categories of data to be able to effectively judge the reliability of the information.

Good data is the fundamental core of all analyses. Having seen a vast number of presentations on the topic of analysis, many companies, even the Fortune 100s, still struggle with getting their data systems to produce accurate and consistent information.

Chapter 6: Analytical Tools

There are quite a few tools available to businesses for data analysis. The higher end tools can be quite expensive and therefore only really an option for the big guys. Additionally, you are usually at the mercy of standardized reporting which means you have few options for customization.

Even when working for the Fortune 100, I preferred to use the less expensive tools to ensure that I had the maximum amount of freedom in my analyses, dashboards and reports. I regarded the big HR systems as large data storage and used them long enough to export the data I needed. After that, I moved on to tools that let me build whatever custom tool or analysis I needed for the business.

If you're not familiar with the names of some of those larger systems, Oracle, PeopleSoft and Success Factors are quite well known but even some of those have provided me with data export challenges and inconveniences.

Data Collection

If you've just entered the world of HR analytics, it won't take long to conclude that the majority of work is in collecting the data and putting it into a usable format. It takes far less time to actually conduct the analysis. You may also spend a good deal of time after the analysis to figure out how to "tell your story." In some of the more urgent analyses, you may simply end up providing a simple yes / no answer to a question like "Did it work?" and then move on to the next analysis.

After twenty years of numerical modeling, I have certainly experienced many of the nuances of the various analysis tools that are out there. The fun thing about trying to select analysis and visualization software for the first time is that it is impossible to truly know the inconveniences of the software until you actually use it. The demo always makes the software look great, doesn't it?

To collect data for an analysis, I prefer the use of Excel and Microsoft Access. Excel is sufficient for smaller amounts of data and Microsoft Access for larger amounts. One of the benefits of Access is that its query capability makes it really easy to store all of your data plus any desired sub-sets of data in one place. Access also tends to run faster than Excel on similar commands.

Because may people are not familiar with Microsoft Access, I have seen them struggle with trying to analyze information with Excel. For larger data sets and the desire to slice-and-dice your data many ways, Excel can be painful. In addition, if you tend to use a lot of pivot tables or VLOOKUP commands in Excel, you will find it gets very slow, very quickly.

It is well worth the effort to learn Access because it contains the ability to create very simple summary queries which would require pivot tables in Excel. These pivot tables will make your file size increase substantially and after several of these tables, the file may become so large that the autosave feature of Excel renders your computer unusable until it finishes. VLOOKUP commands in Excel are a popular way for people to match multiple data sources together, but for larger data sets, you will quickly learn that using Access to match data sets is a better way to go.

Once you have your data set together, depending on your project, you with either elect to use an analysis tool or a visualization tool. Although, as software in the HR space matures, the line between visualization tool and analysis tool is quickly beginning to blur.

Analysis Tools

My favorite pieces of software to use for analysis are MINITAB, SPSS and Tableau. MINITAB, my absolute favourite, is presented as more of an engineer's quality software. However, it includes all of the basic statistical functions, regression analysis functions and time series forecasting which I use for business applications.

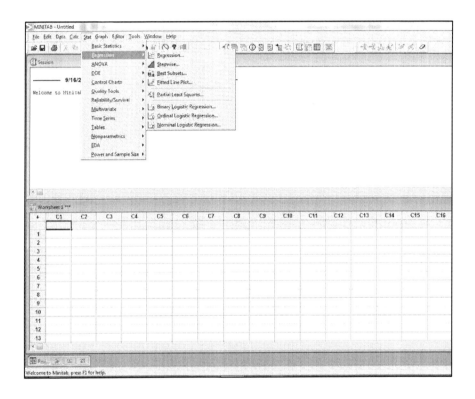

Figure 12: MINTAB Screen

MINITAB has an advantage over SPSS in that it is quite a bit cheaper and once purchased, the licence does not expire. You don't pay again until you want to upgrade to a newer version and for most business applications, there is no need to upgrade each year. At the time of writing this book, the single-licence fee for new users was $1,395 and the upgrade fee was $595. In contrast, in recent years, I paid about $2,700 to get the same capabilities in SPSS and the licence expired in one year. Unless you're using SPSS on a daily basis, there are certainly more cost effective tools to use.

SPSS seems to have additional capabilities that would be of interest to organizational psychologists, but for the most popular types of HR analytics, MINITAB is quite powerful and would be the one tool I would select if I only had sufficient budget for one.

MS Excel, if you install the data analysis add-on, does have statistical functions and regression, but anyone trying to develop a regression model in Excel will quickly find out just how painful it is and how much extra work it creates, especially in cases of multi-variate regression, non-linear applications and repeated regression attempts as you work with your data.

Visualization Tools

These types of tools provide you with a way to display your data and analyses in visually interesting ways for your internal customers. Long gone are the 1990s where we stared at tables of numbers and perhaps a basic graph and attempted to glean what the data was trying to tell us.

The analyst or analytical leader will quickly realize that the market offers two extremes for these tools: fully-customizable or turnkey. The first is best used when you are building user tools that involve aspects that are very specific to your company. For example, I once designed a headcount planning model to predict the operational workforce needed for a transportation company in 30 European countries. Working with the European expert on how the operations functioned, we included factors related to workload drivers, efficiencies, currencies, management spans and several others. The point is, the tool we needed was not something that you would find, or expect to find, in a turnkey solution since it was very specific to how this one company operated.

The second extreme for these tools is obviously the turnkey solution. For reporting and analytics that are common to most companies, a turnkey solution can get you up and running in a lot shorter period of time than developing a home-grown system. Tools in this category have come a long way in just the past few years and are well worth the investment if you are still looking at spreadsheets for your HR information.

Let's take a look at an example of each type. For the fully-customizable analytics tool, I will describe a product called Tableau. As an example of a turnkey solution, we will take a look at a product called Visier.

Tableau allows you to drag your data fields onto a worksheet page to create graphical pages. You can then build dashboard pages by dragging and dropping your graphical pages onto a dashboard page for a more cohesive look at related information.

The new user of Tableau can begin producing visual images very quickly, especially since this tool has a "show me" feature which, based on the data fields selected, it will suggest graph types that make sense for that type of information. A vast number of graph types are available to the user including the ability to overlay data onto map images. This tool automatically detects fields like zip / postal codes, states / provinces, counties and countries to make these map visualizations really easy.

For the more advanced user, this tool can take you into very high levels of complexity if you dare to push it as far as it can go.

If you're thinking that graphs in Excel are good enough, Tableau has a huge advantage over Excel in that you can create live filters on the graphs that you can select and deselect and the graphs will change instantly. In Excel, you would have to create separate graphs for each of these options. Pivot graphs have some of these capabilities in Excel but they are painful to use and what it displays looks less than impressive to your internal customers.

As an example, suppose your management has requested a visualization of time-to-hire results across the country. You can certainly use Excel to create a graph showing the time-to-hire for each geographical area. However, while presenting this to management, they now ask you to show them only the results of time-to-hire for recruiters who have been with the company for less than one year.

With Excel, it's back to the office to create more graphs. With Tableau, you can overlay a filter (in this case for years of service) and with the click of a mouse, the graph instantly changes. As an added bonus, if you had four graphs on a dashboard page in Tableau, changing the selections in the filter list would change all four charts at once. It's an analyst's dream!

As far as purchasing options for this software, Tableau offers a desktop version which will allow you to connect to data sources like Excel and Access for about $1,000.

There is a professional version of this program which will connect to higher end databases which costs just less than $2,000. The annual maintenance fee was $400 at the time of writing this book.

There is a server version of Tableau, but from my experience, purchasing a server and licences was fairly cost prohibitive for many companies so Tableau's recent cloud offering is quite welcome. It eliminates the need to purchase a server which was the majority of cost associated with trying to make dashboards available throughout one's company. At the time of writing, Tableau offered this version for $500/user/year.

Regardless of which visualization tool you eventually purchase, ensure that you can test out a trial version of the software before you make a commitment. I recommend looking at and trying several with a real data set from your company.

Internet research turns up several competitors for the Tableau product which we can divided into traditional BI (Business Intelligence) vendors and data visualization vendors.

Players in the traditional BI vendor space are: SAP, IBM, SAS, Oracle, Microstrategy, and Microsoft. These tend to be behind on Data Visualization (DV) and are less user-friendly. These also tend to require a higher level of investment which may not be possible for many organizations.

Players in the data visualization category are: Qlikview, Spotfire, Tableau, Omniscope, SpreadsheetWEB, Panorama, Advizor Solutions, Actuate (one of the few successful open source vendors), Panopticon, Vizubi (Excel-based), Pentaho, Dundas, and Visual Mining. The web sites for most of these products do not display the price.

Spotfire seems most similar to Tableau in its visualization techniques but the fact that it integrates with Matlab gives a hint that they haven't quite entered the HR space. The focus of their case studies seems to be manufacturing and pharmaceutical.

Another point to keep in mind when investigating software solutions is to determine your analysis needs and approach and then select a tool which meets your needs. Don't purchase an analysis tool and then try to force your analysis approach to meet the tool.

Now let's take a look at the other extreme which was the turnkey solution. As previously mentioned, turnkey solutions are great for reports and analytics that are common to most companies. One such tool which has been created with an HR focus, is Visier.

Most solutions require you to handle the necessary data, analytics tools, visualizations and HR expertise separately. Visier rolls all of this into a single application and is available through the cloud.

There are many advantages to this type of turnkey solution. The first is the speed of deployment. A typical deployment for a traditional business intelligence (BI) tool requires months of data alignment and then further months of building the dashboards and reports that the business will use. Products like Visier allow you to be up and running with workforce analytics that serve the whole business in 4-6 weeks.

BI implementations typically require a great deal of support from IT to build servers, integrate systems, deploy and maintain software. The IT support requirement with a turnkey solution is considerably less, giving HR more independence in how they manage their workforce analytics solution.

There are additional advantages to using systems like this. The analytics modules of HRIS systems like Workday or SuccessFactors only allow you to analyze the data they have in their database.

Visier can absorb information from multiple HR systems, such as Peoplesoft or Workday for employee data and Taleo for recruiting data, and then provide you with a solution that links the multiple data sets. A practical example of this is being able to analyze performance and promotion outcomes from the core employee data, sorted or filtered by the hiring lead source or recruiter from the recruitment data. These are the types of full cycle talent questions HR has been trying to answer for years. It comes pre-built into this application.

The fact that Visier supports multiple data feeds and is application agnostic means that you can build, maintain, and enhance your workforce analytics without being tied to a particular core HR system. You can also change your system without halting or losing any of your analytics outputs.

Visier comes populated with over 300 metrics, analysis tools, visual reporting tools, dashboards and collaboration tools. There is also a unique module which provides guided analysis to HR business partners or line managers, freeing up the time of HR analysts to focus on the strategic questions rather than outputting headcount and turnover reports repeatedly. This module contains best practice answers to core HR questions and includes some predictive elements such as probability of exit and predictors of top talent.

The user interface has been designed to be intuitive which is helpful when it comes to quick adoption across the business.

Visier's solution costs 10-20 times less than a custom BI implementation. Unlike most BI tools which price by user, Visier prices based on current headcount and does not limit the number of people who can access the system. Given HR's role to enable the whole business to make better people decisions, this pricing structure can bring cost advantages as the sophistication and scope of your workforce analytics program increases.

Now that you have heard of at least one product on each end of the spectrum, I am certain that enough information has been presented here in order for you to form a list of questions, do your homework and find a solution that fits your business.

Chapter 7: Strategic Workforce Planning

The dynamics of a global economy and the rapid pace at which it changes have made strategic workforce planning (SWP) one of the "most sought after skills in HR today." This topic has received an increased executive focus as companies attempt to mitigate workforce risk in an uncertain economy and deal with the "challenges of change." You will learn in this chapter, not only a quick overview of workforce planning but also the role that HR analytics plays in this process.

There are many statistics supporting the urgency of this topic. One of the most insightful is the fact that "60% of the jobs in the 21st century require skills possessed by 20% of the workforce" i.e., job skills and competencies required in the future are changing faster than the skills training being provided.

Currently, strategic workforce planning in industry is looking primarily at supply, demand and the quantitative gap between them. The ability to judge the readiness of employees and the ability to project changing competency needs is in its infancy but definitely progressing. With changes occurring as quickly as they are today, strategic workforce planning becomes even more essential.

Strategic workforce planning is a proactive approach which plans to provide:

- the right number of people,
- with the right skill sets,
- in the right location,
- at the right time,
- at the right cost

to ensure successful completion of business objectives. In some definitions you may see the first two bullets captured as "the right people" but I like to clarify that the right people actually means the right number with the right skills.

The five major steps in the **Strategic workforce planning** process are:

- Determine the roles of interest,
- Establish the current state and historical trends,
- Determine desired forecasting scenarios,
- Perform gap assessments,
- Establish action plans.

The Purpose of Strategic Workforce Planning

Strategic workforce planning is about defining the workforce that can execute the organization's strategy, now and in the future. It answers questions such as:

- What are the impacts of demographic shifts and external factors? External factors can include market trends, technology changes, new competency needs, social changes etc.
- What new roles and competencies are needed in the workforce today and in the future?
- What is the gap between supply and demand of talent?
- How can we ensure that the right people are in the right jobs with the right skills at the right time for the right cost?
- Do we build or buy talent to meet our needs?
- Can our planning react quickly enough when conditions change?
- Knowing all of the above, what actions are needed to fulfill the strategic workforce planning goals in order to support the organization's strategy?

The Framework

If you are looking for the official framework for strategic workforce planning, there isn't one. There are almost as many frameworks as there are companies doing strategic workforce planning. Personally, I use my own 5-step framework as I have found it flexible enough to work for multiple company structures and sizes. It also has the benefit that it is easy to explain to people both inside and outside of human resources. My recommendation is to think about how your business operates and to modify the framework to best suit your company.

The framework I developed for my own use is shown in Figure 13. I will begin with a high level description of the process and then present the specific activities for each of the five steps. Again, for those readers desiring more detailed information, I recommend the book described in the Appendix, "Strategic Workforce Planning: Guidance & Back-up Plans."

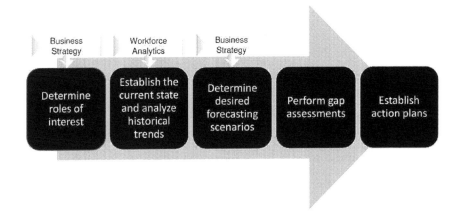

Figure 13: Strategic Workforce Planning Framework

The goal in developing this framework was to keep it as simple as possible for ease of communication to the company's leadership and employees. You can quickly see where HR analytics plays its largest role in workforce planning.

One important point to make is that strategic workforce planning cannot be done without the connection to the business strategy. The frameworks which do not demonstrate this connection run the risk of strategic workforce planning being interpreted as a stand-alone function.

The Role of Business Strategy

As mentioned above, strategic workforce planning must be driven by the business strategy. It cannot succeed in isolation. However, that's not to say that you can't put some portion of the workforce planning process in place while establishing the link to the business strategy, especially if you find yourself implementing workforce planning from the bottom up.

Workforce planning should begin with a clear statement of the business strategy. The business strategy generates the business plan which in most companies is a 3-5 year outlook. This business strategy takes into account items such as the forecasted economic conditions, the impact of possible political uncertainties and elections, market and industry conditions, changing technologies and possible changes in regulations. Health care changes in the U.S. are a good example of regulatory changes impacting organizations. Economic instability in Europe and slowing growth in China are certainly economic conditions affecting most global businesses.

If the strategic workforce planning lead in an organization has "a seat at the table" when the business plan is discussed and finalized, their participation level will vary based on their overall business expertise and how well HR has been integrated into the company. Being in the room, HR can begin thinking about the impacts the strategy will have on the workforce. All is not lost if HR is not in the room for this planning activity. HR just needs to be well-informed about the strategic direction of the company.

Looking at the workforce planning framework, there are two main steps where the business strategy drives the workforce planning activities. In the first step of the framework, we determine the roles of interest. The business strategy determines which roles within the organization are critical to the successful execution of the strategy and critical to the organization's future. I will discuss this step in more detail shortly.

In Step 3 of the framework, the business strategy is what determines the desired forecasting scenarios. Recall that the strategy development included all of the environmental considerations (business environment) in order to create the list of "possible futures."

How does knowledge of the business strategy then translate into the people strategy? Here is one example. Knowing how your company makes money will guide you to the jobs that are most crucial in generating revenue. This would be discovered in the role segmentation step. Knowing these positions, is there a good pipeline of candidates for these jobs? This pipeline can be internal or external. Recognizing that this pipeline is important to the future of the business, your people plans may include talent development plans, training plans and recruitment plans to maintain this pipeline.

Let's take a look at another example. What are the key business objectives for your company for the next 5 years? Is there a large shift in skill sets needed for your future? If so, can you develop these new competencies in your existing workforce or do you need to locate external candidates? If you develop the skills in-house, will that leave vacancies in the employee base as you migrate the employees into this new role? If you can't develop your current employees into this new role, is there a group of employees who become obsolete? The answer to all of these questions will drive the specific actions in your people plans.

Now that we've covered the role that business strategy plays in the strategic workforce planning process, let's take a look at the specific steps.

The Five Steps of Workforce Planning

Step 1: Determine the Roles of Interest

The roles of interest in an organization are the ones required to successfully accomplish the strategic objectives. In some companies, these positions are referenced as critical or pivotal. I have several reasons for avoiding those terms as they tend to impact behaviour.

Strategic objectives are defined by the business strategy. Looking at the roles in an organization, why do we begin workforce planning by segmenting the roles or determining roles of interest?

For most companies, there would be little value in dedicating strategic workforce planning resources to analyzing roles that are not critical or pivotal to your company. Therefore this step is designed to focus the efforts of the strategic workforce planning staff on roles that matter the most and where changes to those roles yield the most value.

For those readers interested in detailed information on a variety of methods to execute this step, the book, Strategic Workforce Planning described in the appendix provides multiple methods. These methods can be as simple as dividing job roles into four categories related to how closely they tie to the execution of the business strategy or as complicated as assessing connections of the role to the competitive advantage of the company.

It should be noted that this activity is not just of value to strategic workforce planning. It can also be used as a prioritization method for HR activities and offerings.

Step 2: Establish the Current State

Establishing the current state is not just about today. It's also very important to know how you got there. What significant business events occurred in the past? Which of these events will impact the future? What trends do you see? This type of information will become even more significant in the next step of the framework when projecting modeling data forward.

Step 3: Determine Desired Forecasting Scenarios

This step involves determining and running desired scenarios of the future. Since there are always business uncertainties (markets, industries, environments, technology changes, etc.), scenario planning is essentially a tool used for making better business decisions in relation to possible uncertainties.

Suppose you anticipate growing your business by 10% in the next year. If you planned for this one scenario, you would have no room for error. What happens if your business only grows by 2%? Perhaps it may grow by 15%? How will that impact your business? How will that impact your human capital plan? Do you have enough flexibility in your workforce to handle all of these cases? What if your revenue is declining?

For these reasons, scenario planning is not a pure science. It comes down to a combination of data analysis, research regarding areas of uncertainty and experience.

Determining the predictions for the desired scenarios is also included in this step and several methods can be used. A simple headcount forecast can be used using Excel based on past trends in the case where a company is in more of a "steady as she goes" stage. A more in-depth forecast model can be built using a determination of the workload drivers for the company. In this type of forecast, the factors affecting workload for each primary job role are established and those factors are used to determine the quantity of resources needed in the future. Cost of the workforce is also established in addition to a variety of tracking metrics.

Step 4: Perform Gap Assessments

In a previous phase of the data evolution, we would have considered only the gap in the headcount we have today and what we need in the immediate future. In strategic workforce planning, there are two types of gaps. The first gap is indeed the gap in headcount although the timespan is probably three to five years instead of the short term. The second gap is where the process gets a lot more involved since we assess the gap between the competencies we have today and the competencies we need in the future.

Step 5: Establish Action Plans

This final step determines the action plans which will close the gaps identified in the previous steps. These plans could involve almost any area of the business. If the gap is one of headcount only, the action plan may involve recruitment. If the gap is one of skill sets, it may involve the training team.

This is the step where a company would establish not only the plans, but also look into more than one plan option. The cost of the options would be investigated and the strategic benefits of each of them. Do you hire internally or contract additional employees? Do you build the talent or buy it? Will the investment of cash produce a return?

Chapter 8: Implementation

From extensive benchmarking, it is clear that it will take at least a year to add a functioning HR analytics team into an organization that has no HR analytics capabilities today. It requires hiring the right talent, communicating the capabilities of the team, investigation and resolution of data issues, the possible creation of new data sources, establishing the best technologies to support the team, researching HRIS systems and establishing internal relationships. The list goes on.

However, a company can begin to see the value that data insights can provide from launching the first few analytical "quick wins" to its internal customers. This tends to drive interest in the topic more than any internal marketing on the subject.

Selling the Concept

If you traditionally rely on statistics from outside of your own company to guide the decisions you make in HR, there is an inherent danger in assuming that the issues presented by others are the same issues affecting your own business. That's not to say that you should ignore information from other sources, but certainly validate that it is applicable to your company.

HR Analytics in some companies begins with the presentation of a business case to the leadership in order to gain support for the initiative. You can certainly use outside statistics to support your business case for building an analytics team but be sure to communicate to your leadership that these are guidelines supporting the urgency of building an analytics team and that you will be analyzing the data of your own company for decision-making purposes. Otherwise, they will see no need to add this function to HR. The business case should also be very specific to your company's challenges and not just a general presentation of public survey results as your justification. What problems are stressing the company today? Which of those can be investigated if you had access to HR analytics?

Another challenge in creating your business case may reside within the HR leader. Some companies embarking on the HR analytics initiative have selected an existing member of Human Resources to lead the effort. This leader may not have the business acumen or a sufficient understanding of the business strategy to build an effective case. In this case, interviewing your business leaders to learn their challenges would be valuable.

Your business case should also contain a list of benefits to be gained from HR analytics. I have stated quite a few benefits throughout this book and the list of practical examples shown earlier should allow you to demonstrate specific ways to provide value and cost savings to the company.

My final piece of advice is to order your business case justifications such that the largest impact items are presented first. Nothing grabs the attention of your leadership like references to large dollar impacts. This will get the attention of your audience. Don't over-estimate the benefits as you will certainly be questioned later if you fall far short of your promises.

The Challenges

Quite a few companies have been on the path to establishing HR analytics teams over recent years. That's not to say that analytics is new but, as we have seen, it has not been a large focus in Human Resources until recent years. People like me, with numerical backgrounds, were not usually found in Human Resources. The world now competes on information and knowing the analytical relationships between the aspects of your business will allow HR and the business to make wiser decisions.

Having compared practices with many of these companies, every single one has experienced their own challenges. Some challenges we all have in common and some are unique. The following is a presentation of some of the more common challenges, keeping in mind that many companies start by "selling the business case for analytics."

In the previous section, we addressed the need to ensure that the business case was specific to your own company and not a general argument for analytics. Even with a well-prepared business case, you may still fail to get the support of leadership.

The following section presents information and advice for HR analytics leaders on how to move forward with these challenges. The following challenges are presented:

- Culture,
- Vision,
- Budget,
- Leadership support,
- Data issues,
- Legal issues,
- Company size, and
- Acceptance of results.

Culture

Culture has a huge impact on the successful implementation of an HR analytics team. Given that the first step most people take is to sell the business case to gain support for adding these capabilities, you would benefit from an open-minded, progressive leadership. If they are not progressive and have perhaps grown stale in the position, then they have probably seen business cases for a variety of initiatives presented to them for years. The challenge in this case is to convince the leadership that your business case is so much more important to the future of the company than the others they are seeing.

If you don't manage to sell the business case for HR analytics, here is some guidance on how you can proceed.

You did your research, you created a fabulous business plan, you communicated the plan to your management and then it didn't get approved. That's okay. Perhaps the company can't afford the cost of implementing an entire analytics team. Perhaps your leadership has seen so many business cases that they have become numb to them. Perhaps your leadership feels that the company has done so well for so long that they see no need to spend money on putting analytical experts inside Human Resources. What do you do now?

My advice in this situation is to begin with what you can. Which low cost items can you implement and still show immediate value, especially in terms of saving money? It has been my experience that having specific results to show which address a specific problem will yield greater support.

Vision

Some people have difficulty envisioning new concepts until you show them specific examples. After several of these examples, you will find that people will start to come to you with new requests. After demonstrating some key linkages in one company, I began to get enquiries from global locations wanting the same types of analyses.

Of course, ensure that the data system you use for your first few, high-value examples is reliable enough to conduct a valid analysis. Nothing will kill your effort faster than a bad analysis right out of the starting gate.

Budget

You may very well find yourself in the situation where your leadership is sold on the concept, but cannot back it financially. Most companies who have succeeded in selling the concept and have obtained the financial backing have set up a central group to run HR analytics or have added HR analytics professionals into a central strategy team.

A second challenge in the area of resources is the readiness of HR to guide the discussions on linking HR to the business.

Leadership Support

Suppose the top leadership supports and funds the concept of HR analytics. To be successful, you now need to work with the head of each division or sub-organization to be successful. It is possible that not all of these people "wish to play." Some leaders will become rather guarded if HR analytics is entering his / her area for the first time for fear of what it will reveal. Don't let these leaders distract you from your goal. Focus on the willing participants first.

When you approach the business unit or division leader with the concept of HR analytics, it may be perceived as an HR activity solely for the benefit of HR. Approach HR analytics from the point of view that you are providing a service to your internal customer.

Again, selling the concept of HR as the facilitator for the purpose of meeting the internal customer's needs is the mindset you need to stress.

Data Issues

We discussed quite a few challenges with data in a previous chapter, so I won't go into too much detail here, but for those who skipped ahead in this book, some of the more popular challenges with data were:

- Awareness of the data systems,
- Access to data systems,
- Missing data,
- Unknown definitions,
- Technology challenges, and
- Acceptance of results.

Legal Issues

For some companies, legal structure is an issue. Depending on the legal entities involved, it is sometimes forbidden to exchange data between the legal entities or even to leverage resources across the company lines. There is not much you can do about this challenge beyond recognizing that it exists and do what you can within the legal guidelines.

Company Size

It is sometimes advantageous to be a small company rather than a large corporation because it is easier to collect the cross-functional leaders together for collaborative discussions. These leaders are likely more familiar with each other and act more as a team. In larger corporations, the leaders may be so far removed from each other functionally and geographically that they see less need to operate across the silos.

Planning

Implementation planning for HR analytics can get quite involved. It is difficult to log all of the considerations that go into creating a successful plan.

- How will we communicate the capabilities that we are selling?

- Which issues should we address first to demonstrate the value of HR analytics?
- How will we establish the relationships we need across the company?

Beyond relationships, communications and demonstrating value, you need to establish data and technology plans, namely,

- How will we assess our current data sources?
- Are our current metrics the right ones?
- Do we have the right technology and tools?

An additional planning aspect is centered around reporting. How often should this information be generated? How well can we standardize the information across our array of customers? It is unlikely that the needs across the company will be the same.

Remember that executives don't know what they need when it comes to HR analytics. It is very new to them. It is the role of the HR analytics leader to guide these executives to the analysis projects which allow them to make solid, data-driven decisions. It is also the role of this leader to communicate the linkages which can be found within HR and between HR and the business. A leader outside of HR is not going to think about why he needs to assess the linkage between engagement and turnover.

At this point, it might be a good idea to create a checklist of the implementation components you will need for your own company and prioritize them. What is in existence today that you can leverage to move ahead faster and show "quick wins?" What subject matter experts do you have access to that have been down this path before you? Which professional network groups can you access for advice?

With the vast number of questions proposed in consideration for implementing HR analytics, I am certain that this section has provided a clear picture of what may be involved in implementing a new HR analytics function in an organization. Thought, discussion, planning, organization and execution are what matter most.

Chapter 9: Concluding Remarks

HR analytics is helping to transform Human Resources from being a tactical support function into a strategic partner. While analytics is not new in other functional areas of the business, it is fuelling rapid change in HR.

Skill sets never seen in HR before are beginning to appear. New HR vendors are showing up on the market to address a new need. Previously disparate systems are beginning to merge.

The need for greater understanding of HR data and the relationships hidden deeply therein will provide HR with the capability to provide greater value to the organization. Not only will HR be able to understand the connection between measurements like engagement and turnover, but they will also be able to quantify the impact of one on the other. As more of these connections are determined, HR can begin to map the mathematical dependencies that exist within its department and expand outward to their internal customers. Several practical examples of these connections have been provided in this book in order to paint a clear picture of the possibilities.

A recommendation to analysts for how to remain organized when planning an analysis has been provided in a simple five step approach. In addition, some guidelines for selecting the right metrics for your organization have been outlined.

A brief outline of the workforce planning process has been provided and its link to HR analytics demonstrated. As two of the hottest topics in HR today, these two functions complement each other well in their ability to drive Human Resources in a strategic direction.

Many of the top implementation challenges facing HR Analytics leaders have been described and advice provided on how to attempt to overcome these challenges. The thought process of HR is evolving in this regard and providing clear benefits in your first few analyses will help to speed up how HR thinks about decision-making. For those implementing strategic workforce planning at the same time as HR analytics, you will find the challenges of implementation to be very similar.

Additional advice has been provided on which skill sets to look for when trying to build an in-house analytics team. These skill sets cover both the analytical and communication needs.

The book also provided an overview of the types of tools available on the market for HR analytics. These tools range from data collection to analysis to visualization. For the latter two categories, we are also beginning to see some tools do both, at least at the basic level. From the turn-key solution to the fully-customizable dashboard builder, there is a tool out there for almost any skill and budget level.

It is my hope that I have provided you with a sufficient enough overview of HR analytics and its value to the organization, that you are confident enough to embark on the journey yourself. Or, if you are a student wondering whether the world of analytics is for you, I hope I have convinced you that this is a worthy area to study. Analytics now exists in every area of the company and the need for analytical talent is on the rise.

Welcome to HR analytics...

Numerical Insights on the Web

Looking to find out more about Numerical Insights and what we can do for your company? We offer the following services:

- On-site corporate workshops to teach your HR team to use analytics and strategic workforce planning,
- Speaking engagements,
- Personalized consulting services on HR analytics and workforce planning, and
- On-call advice for business leaders looking to learn more about analytics.

You can find us on the web at **www.numericalinsights.com**. Our web site contains a sign-up newsletter list if you wish to be notified of future publications or information regarding analytics.

You can reach us by email at: **publications@numericalinsights.com**

You can also follow Tracey on the web using Facebook or Twitter.

Facebook: http://www.facebook.com/numericalinsights

Twitter ID: @NInsights

Appendix A: Other Publications by the Author

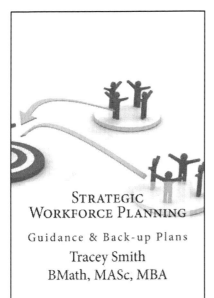

Tracey is the author of **Strategic Workforce Planning: Guidance & Back-Up Plans.**

Strategic workforce planning aims to proactively put the right people, in the right place, at the right time at the right cost in order to mitigate workforce risk now and in the future.

The dynamics of a global economy have made strategic workforce planning one of the "most sought after skills in Human Resources today."

This book will:

- Teach you the framework of strategic workforce planning,
- Provide you with multiple implementation approaches,
- Outline how to successfully sell the concept and tell you what to do when selling the concept fails,
- Demonstrate ideas for measuring success,
- Clarify the connection to other HR functions,
- Discuss how to define the roles and responsibilities,

- Show you practical tools and approaches for successful implementation, and
- Outline the major challenges facing strategic workforce planning leaders today.

This book has sold throughout the U.S., Canada, Europe, the U.K., and Asia. Here are a few reader comments from around the world:

"I have read the book and am really enlightened by the author's thoughts and writings. The author is one of the best practitioners in this field. Her approach on workforce planning is very practical and useful. The book gives me a lot of Aha moments. I have learnt a lot and will surely apply them in my future work."

"Just finished reading Strategic Workforce Planning. It was outstanding, and very practical. You clearly know what you're writing about, and practitioners in the workforce planning space would find your book a worthwhile contribution to the body of knowledge. I wish you great success with the book. I do plan to order and read Data Driven Decision Making for Small Businesses."

"The book lays out all the fundamental things you need to consider when you develop a strategic workforce plan. I especially like the fact that several examples were provided."

"This is a great overview of the subject of Strategic Workforce Planning, with a heavy focus on the important 'Strategy' part. Direct and to the point, it clearly lays out the author's preferred process, and offers advice on how to implement in your own company. She

does this in simple terms without a lot of math. I would recommend this book for those companies that are starting their journey and are looking for where to start."

"I've been through a number of workshops, formal training events related to SWP and have always come away with a different perspective or tool to use for the groups I support as a business partner. Tracey's book feels real ... and I got the sense of [reality] from the business leader perspective as well as the SWP facilitator."

Appendix B: HR Analytics Blogs

Tracey Smith's articles and blogs are followed by a worldwide audience. The following materials are reprints of several blogs written after the original publication of this book. They are provided for the interest of the reader.

Did You Check the Box on HR Analytics?

A good deal of HR analytics is about studying trends and investigating the driving forces behind those trends. I've noticed a new trend in the HR analytics world and it has nothing to do with the actual numbers.

I was providing advice to someone who was in charge of implementing HR analytics within her company. I recommended carefully selecting metrics which align to the future direction of the business and specific company challenges. This would provide the greatest value to her internal customers. After a few exchanges of information, this person said "I'm just going to pick a bunch metrics, make a dashboard and see what happens from there." This is what I call "checking the box on HR analytics." It provides little value to your internal customers since there is no thought behind the selection of metrics. You risk distributing a dashboard that no one will use and you risk your reputation as a knowledgeable analytics professional.

In speaking with a young professional in another company, he shared that he was told to "...just provide any metrics you think are important" without explanation for the need. Being greatly concerned with this approach, he embarked on a personally driven mission to interview his internal customers to identify concerns with the workforce. He will then select his metrics to align to those concerns. We must commend this individual for not "checking the HR analytics box" and we should be disappointed with the leadership who instructed him.

There are others that throw large sums of money at the topic to implement HR analytics software. These packages are great at consolidating data in companies where data has not been collected or is spread so far apart in the company that it is not feasible to put it together manually for strategic studies. These packages may identify trends, but they will not provide insights into what is truly happening in the business. You still need someone with the expertise to "see" what the data may be telling you on a deeper level.

If your HR Analytics function doesn't provide value to the business, why does it exist? Check the box or spend a little more time thinking about which metrics and studies would provide value to the organization. As analytics professionals and leaders, the choice is up to you. One choice will move you forward; the other will hold you back.

Big Data: Still Confused?

Outside of HR, "big data" has been defined as large, complex data sets which make computation and analysis difficult. So what does that mean? How large is large? As computational power continues to increase, the definition of "large" must surely move along with it. Do I reach "large" when I exceed the row limits in Excel? Microsoft Access? When I can no longer run my statistical software? Do I reach "large" when I can no longer use a PC or laptop for computation?

In viewing a conference session recently, a panel of experts was asked to define what "big data" meant to them. The definitions varied widely. Several defined it as information that couldn't be processed on one machine or data which was "bigger than you can count." If a machine can count it but a human can't, was it countable? Others placed less emphasis on the volume of data and referenced combing multiple data sets to provide the foundation for an analysis not previously performed.

Here's my opinion on the topic. I actually don't dedicate any time deciding how I would like to define "big data." As an analytics professional, it matters very little to me how we define this term or whether we use that term at all. Like several on the panel, I agree that what matters is what you do with the data you have and the strategic business decisions you make as a result. I've performed many analyses with no more than 100,000 records and managed to use this information to make recommended changes in HR processes and offerings. With a data set of less than 200 records, I recommended halting an HR program because it wasn't effective. With a data set of less than 2,000 records, I managed to predict the future workforce needed to meet the forthcoming demands by increased revenue plans. I know there are many analytics professionals out there who can cite similar projects. For those who know me, my background was Engineering and then Supply Chain before it was HR. Regardless of the functional area, the value in data remains the same. What decisions did the analysis of data allow you to make to move the business forward? This value is what matters.

As simply stated as those examples were, don't take that simplicity to mean the analysis work was trivial. It still involved a good deal of work cleaning and merging data sets before any analysis could take place. But those of us in the analytical world know that 75% of the work in any analysis project usually resides in the data preparation. In contrast, the hardest part of any analysis is in the interpretation of the results in terms of what it means to the business.

So for those confused about all the hype in the HR world around "big data," don't worry. Put that confusion aside and dedicate your thoughts to analyses which can be performed in order to make decisions of value.

One Size Does Not Fit All

As some of you may know, my approach to solving HR problems is customized. I do not guide customers into standardized templates and software. When I attend conferences, I am almost always asked which software I selected for an analytics or workforce planning solution when I led the effort for a global Fortune 100 company. My answer is, "none." I thought I would take this opportunity to provide some insight into my reasoning.

While analytics and workforce planning applications are making progress, I found none that would convince me that the cost of the software would be less than the value I could derive from performing customized and targeted studies. The latter yields higher value. None of the applications had capabilities anywhere near what I could perform on my own. Yes, I admit it... my high value and strategic work was performed with Excel, Access and a data visualization package. There's nothing wrong with that. Every single workforce planning model I have ever built has been different. I build these models to provide insight into the specific issues related to a particular company's issues. Even within the same company, the issues vary by job role, geography etc., so the models are constructed to look at the workforce data in different ways. Large software applications lock you into viewing information in the same way as your competitor. Where is the strategic advantage in purchasing expensive software which aims to make you the same as your competitor? Competitive advantage comes from being different.

Now, if you find that your data systems are a mess and highly dispersed, then some of these applications may serve as a good, centralized source of information and will give you basic trending. That's a good start but the value in HR analytics is in delving deeper to determine the root cause of the trending you see.

If you are blessed with fairly good data systems like I was previously, it wasn't all that painful to pull information from multiple systems across global regions and use a program like Microsoft Access to construct the data source needed for a specific analysis. Additionally, for trend analyses in HR, it is unlikely that you need your data to be real time. You are more likely to be studying how things are changing in your workforce over months or years rather than days. For workforce planning, it is about planning the workforce you need within, say, the next three to five years, not tomorrow. Also, workforce planning generally hones in on specific job roles instead of taking an in-depth look at all employees.

As admitted by one software vendor on a webcast I attended, these vendors are struggling with their customers being able to find value in their product. I think you will find that the ones that found value were likely extracting information from the system and performing customized analyses with the data. Those that aren't finding value probably thought that implementing an HR analytics or workforce planning solution would magically reveal deep insights into their workforce.

36249228R00073

Made in the USA
Lexington, KY
11 October 2014